FEUDALISM, MONARCHIES, AND NOBILITY

FEUDALISM, MONARCHIES, AND NOBILITY

Edited by Jeanne Nagle

Britannica®
Educational Publishing

IN ASSOCIATION WITH

ROSEN
EDUCATIONAL SERVICES

Published in 2015 by Britannica Educational Publishing (a trademark of Encyclopædia Britannica, Inc.) in association with The Rosen Publishing Group, Inc.
29 East 21st Street, New York, NY 10010

Distributed exclusively by Rosen Publishing.
To see additional Britannica Educational Publishing titles, go to rosenpublishing.com.

First Edition

Britannica Educational Publishing
J.E. Luebering: Director, Core Reference Group
Anthony L. Green: Editor, Compton's by Britannica

Rosen Publishing
Hope Lourie Killcoyne: Executive Editor
Jeanne Nagle: Editor
Nelson Sá: Art Director
Michael Moy: Designer
Cindy Reiman: Photography Manager
Marty Levick: Photo Researcher

Cataloging-in-Publication Data

Feudalism, monarchies, and nobility/edited by Jeanne Nagle.—First Edition.
      pages cm.—(Political and economic systems)
Includes bibliographical references and index.
ISBN 978-1-62275-347-5 (library bound)
1.   Feudalism—Juvenile   literature.   2.   State,   The—Juvenile   literature.
3. Civilization, Medieval—Juvenile literature. I. Nagle, Jeanne.
JC111.F468 2014
321'.3—dc23

                                                                        2014007484

Manufactured in the United States of America

On the cover, p. 3: *Culture Club/Hulton Archive/Getty Images*

CONTENTS

54

67

85

92

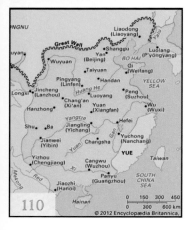

110

117

130

A medieval serf plows a field, as other peasants prune trees in an orchard in the middle ground. This illuminated manuscript image is from the 15th-century Très Riches Heures du Duc de Berry, *a book of hours (devotional prayer book) created by the Limbourg brothers of the Netherlands.* The Bridgeman Art Library/Getty Images

INTRODUCTION

When it comes to matters of economics, people often refer to the "haves" and "have-nots." There is a clear distinction between people with wealth and privilege and those who do menial work just to feed themselves and their families.

As stark as those contrasts may seem today, in past centuries these separate economic tiers were even farther apart and, for the most part, inescapable. The feudal system, which predominated in Europe during the Middle Ages, formalized these class distinctions. (Though the timing and details varied, similar systems developed in other parts of the world as well.) In fact, supported by various monarchies and the aristocracy that benefited from the arrangement, the feudal system divided people politically and socially as well as economically. This book examines the ramifications of life under feudal constructs, including both the privileges enjoyed by nobility and the hardships suffered by peasants and serfs.

Despite the inherent unfairness of a such social systems, considering the status of serfs and lords in a historical context makes it apparent that they did have a role to play in the economic development of nations. Examining how systems such as feudalism and the aristocracy came into existence and what role they played can help provide an understanding of why they became so widespread. Looking at the huge gap between the extravagant lifestyles of the privileged and the harsh existence of the peasantry also provides some clue as to why the feudal system did not last and why monarchies and the nobility have declined significantly in importance.

"Feudalism" is a term used to describe a system centered around three broad classes: wealthy landowners who dominated economic, military, and legal control of their localities;

vassals who performed various services or provided payment to the landowners in exchange for the right to farm part of their land; and serfs who were bound to work on specific properties with little compensation or freedom of movement. Various forms of feudal systems developed throughout Europe and in parts of Asia, to different degrees and at different times. In western Europe, the system was prominent from the 5th century through the 12th century. It is important to understand that in a society that had limited communication from place to place and has left few surviving written records, descriptions of feudalism are generalizations that may not apply precisely to each specific situation and which may have been influenced by various historical biases in the subsequent centuries. In any case, feudalism can be looked at as an economic model that broadly represents a system in which centralized power was weak, allowing local lords to exercise a great deal of control over how the ordinary people in their areas lived and worked.

The roots of feudalism can be traced back to the decline of the Roman Empire. Absent the strong authority of the Romans, much of Europe became a fairly wild and lawless place. Given the chaos and violence of the countryside, poor farmers naturally flocked to powerful local lords for protection. Over time, they increasingly gave control of their possessions and livelihoods to those local lords in exchange for that protection, often losing many of their individual freedoms in the process. The powerful landlords, meanwhile, took advantage of the absence of a strong central authority to expand their holdings and tighten their control over the people in their service.

In the Middle Ages, the economy was largely agrarian, so it was natural that the feudal system centred around holdings of land. Landowners would essentially lease the rights to a portion of their lands to vassals. The areas of land so granted were known as fiefs. These vassals could profit from working their fiefs, as long as they met their obligations to the landowners. The poorest class of society was the serfs, who essentially worked just to feed themselves and their families, with no hope of further gain or social mobility.

The distinction between serfs and slaves is a narrow one. Unlike slaves, serfs were technically paid for their work, but they did not have freedom of movement. This meant that serfs were not truly free, and economically it meant that they were stuck with whatever financial terms their landlord dictated, so compensation for their labors was minimal.

Vassals, on the other hand, were more like tenants who generally had freedom of movement, so they could abandon one fief for another if they did not like the landlord's terms. Also, vassals did not necessarily have to work the land to pay their landlords—they could perform other services, such as military service on behalf of the landlord. This is how the concept of knighthood evolved out of feudalism, with the knights essentially being vassals who performed military rather than agricultural services in exchange for the income from their fiefs. In time, not having to work the land gave knights more freedom and higher status than ordinary vassals.

As feudalism developed, increasingly formal rules emerged governing the arrangements between landlords and tenants and the rights of those tenants. These rules varied from place to place. In England and France, for example, there were distinctions between free and unfree tenures, which basically determined the freedom a tenant had to perform services other than farming and leave the fief if he chose to. In China, whose feudal period predated Europe's by centuries, serfs technically had greater freedom than those in Europe, though as a practical matter they generally lacked the means to escape service to their masters. In Japan, allegiances were split between spiritual and military rulers, which often complicated loyalties within that country's feudal system.

Just as specific feudal models had their variations from place to place, the demise of feudalism followed a different pattern in various countries. In general, the strengthening of central governments and periodic peasant uprisings were part of the process. In western Europe, these factors were exacerbated by the Black Death in the 14th century, a massive plague that created a labor shortage, increasing the economic power of the peasants.

In contrast, central monarchies were not as strong in eastern Europe at that time, and a growing demand for grain increased the profit motive for the wealthy to seize peasant lands and exploit their labor. As a result, feudalism lingered much longer in eastern Europe; Russia did not formally grant its serfs freedom until 1861. In Asia, feudalism maintained a strong influence over Japanese culture well into the 19th century, and China did not formally end feudalism until the People's Republic of China was created in 1949.

An economic value of the feudal system was to increase the productivity of the land by organizing individual efforts into broader, though highly localized, economic enterprises. However, since these enterprises were for the benefit of the privileged few at the expense of the generally nonvoluntary efforts of the many, it is easy to see why this model did not last.

If feudalism was based on a formal exercise of class distinctions, monarchy took the idea of a class system to its extreme, placing one person above all others in the state, often based on the claim of a divine right to the position. Monarchy is a system in which supreme power in a state is held by one person, and this position is generally passed on through heredity.

Monarchies are as ancient as the early Chinese, Babylonian, and Egyptian civilizations; and some still exist to this day, though in considerably watered-down form. In Europe, the concept of a centralized monarch ruling a clearly defined territory became prominent around the 12th century, just as feudalism was beginning to decline in many countries. While monarchies and the feudal system overlapped each other to a degree, the strengthening of monarchies—or, rather, a centralized government—represented the beginning of the end for the feudal system.

While monarchies were similar to the feudal system in their reliance on a strictly observed class system, strong centralized monarchies also created some contradictions to the feudal system. Whereas feudalism represented the decentralization of power into the hands of a series of local overlords, monarchy represented the concentration of power into one central ruler. Monarchies also created a higher allegiance for all subjects than their local lords. They also helped build a sense of national identity and, gradually, stronger bodies of law. Each of these factors helped fray the bonds that held serfs and vassals to their lords.

Just as feudalism played the economic role of combining individual efforts into concentrated enterprises, monarchies took the next step in economic development by focusing the people's efforts on national goals such as developing trade, building armies, and expanding empires. In this sense, monarchies helped further organize the efforts of a country, turning a series of local economies into a national one.

Monarchs often ruled with the cooperation of powerful groups, whether formal legislative bodies such as England's Parliament or wealthy landowners who exerted influence in countries such as Russia. In many cases, this led to conflict between the monarch's desire to exercise unlimited power and the self-interest others had in wanting to check or share that power. These conflicts could push a country in one of two directions—toward an absolutist monarchy, as in the case of Catherine the Great of Russia, or toward a weakened monarchy such as that which emerged after the English Civil War of the 17th century.

Besides conflicts with powerful people who wanted to share in a nation's rule, another thing that eroded the concept of monarchy was the growth of secular philosophy in the 17th and 18th centuries. This brought new expressions of individual rights, which did not mesh well with the notion of serving an absolute ruler whose supremacy was the will of God.

The combination of internal conflicts and a greater emphasis on individual rights and equality eventually led to the demise of the monarch as a strong centralized ruler. This end came in different ways in different places—through the gradual concession of power to an elected body, as in England; through popular revolution, as in Russia; or through military defeat, as in Germany's loss during World War I.

Monarchies do still exist in various forms today, but to a much more limited degree than in the 12th through 18th centuries. These limitations may take the form of monarchs having purely ceremonial duties, having to share power with a broader group, or simply having domain over a relatively small kingdom.

The role of the nobility effectively bridges the gap between feudal society and the rise of monarchies. Nobles were originally people who came from long lines of wealthy families or families renowned for great deeds such as military conquest. They were careful to protect the distinction that came with their heritage by marrying among themselves or into other powerful family lines. As with the monarchy, then, the concept of nobility relied heavily on heredity and thus helped underscore the social immobility of the time; it was virtually impossible for a person to move up in class.

Nobles often descended from the powerful land-owning families of feudal times, and beyond that era they continued to use their wealth and position to exert influence. Nobles were often essential in helping to support monarchs, though they were also occasionally instrumental in undermining them. Nobles also served key economic functions, from organizing trade and farming efforts to acting as patrons of the arts. Of course, some nobles were more generous than others, and in many cases their cruelty and selfishness repressed rather than advanced their society.

Eventually, many of the same factors that had weakened monarchies also diminished the power and wealth of the nobility. Partly this was philosophical, as greater self-awareness and belief in individual rights made people less content to be subject to the will of others. Partly, though, the reason for the decline was economic. The economic development that feudalism, monarchies, and the nobility helped to advance eventually led to economies that were more dependent on trade and innovation, which diluted the importance of inherited wealth and, especially, of inherited status. The broader and more efficient communication that came with these more developed economies helped foster the spread of ideas, and eventually these ideas convinced more and more people that feudalism, monarchies, and the nobility had largely outlived their usefulness.

Feudalism, monarchy, and the nobility helped bring some order to civilizations that in many cases were just emerging from the Dark Ages and ultimately transitioned them toward modern economies. One shortcoming of these systems was the failure to share the fruits of this enhanced productivity with most of the people who contributed to it, which gave workers no incentive to continue to support the system. Therefore, while the feudal system once played an important role in history, it was destined to be a temporary one. Studying the rise and decline of feudalism, as well as its connection to and impact on monarchy and the aristocracy, can help bring a greater perspective to understanding conflicts between the haves and have-nots of today's society.

CHAPTER 1

A FEUDALISM OVERVIEW

The historiographic construct known as feudalism has been used most narrowly to describe relations between lords and vassals that involve the exchange of land for military service. In truth, however, a broader definition is more accurate: The feudal system overarchingly defined the social, economic, and political conditions prevalent in western Europe during the early Middle Ages, the long stretch of time between the 5th and 12th centuries.

Feudalism in this sense is thought to have emerged in a time of political disorder in the 11th century as a means to restore order, and it was later a key element in the establishment of strong monarchies. "Feudalism" also has been applied, often inappropriately, to non-Western societies where institutions similar to those of medieval Europe are thought to have existed. The many ways "feudalism" has been used have drained it of specific meaning, however, and caused some scholars to reject it as a useful concept for understanding medieval society.

Defining the Term

"Feudalism" and the related term "feudal system" are labels invented long after the period to which they were applied. They refer to what those who invented them perceived as the most significant and distinctive characteristics of the early and central Middle Ages.

The expressions *féodalité* and "feudal system" were coined by the beginning of the 17th century, and the English words "feudality" and "feudalism" (as well as "feudal pyramid") were in use by the end of the 18th century. They were derived from the Latin words *feudum* ("fief") and *feodalitas* (services connected with the fief), both of which were used during the Middle Ages and later to refer to a form of property holding.

In European feudal society, the fief was a vassal's source of income, held from his lord in exchange for services. The fief constituted the central institution of feudal society. It normally consisted of land to which a number of unfree peasants were attached; the land was supposed to be sufficient to support the vassal and to secure his knight service for the lord. Its size varied greatly, according to the income it could provide. It has been calculated that a fief needed from 15 to 30 peasant families to maintain one knightly household. Fief sizes varied widely, ranging from huge estates and whole provinces to a plot of a few acres. Besides land, dignities and offices and money rents were also given in fief.

Use of the terms associated with *feudum* to denote the essential characteristics of the early Middle Ages has invested the fief with exaggerated prominence and placed undue emphasis on the importance of a special mode of land tenure to the detriment of other, more significant aspects of social, economic, and political life.

Origins of the Idea

The terms "feudalism" and "feudal system" were generally applied to the early and central Middle Ages. This was the period from the 5th century, when central political authority in the Western empire disappeared, to the 12th century, when kingdoms began to emerge as effective centralized units of government.

For a relatively brief period, from the mid-8th to the early 9th century, the Carolingian rulers, especially Pippin (reigned 751–768) and Charlemagne (reigned 768/771–814), had remarkable success in creating and maintaining a relatively unified empire. Before and afterward, however, political units were fragmented and political authority diffused. The mightier of the later Carolingians attempted to regulate local magnates and enlist them in their service, but the power of local elites was never effaced. In the absence of forceful kings and emperors, local lords expanded the territory subject to them and intensified their control over the people living there.

In many areas the term *feudum*, as well as the terms *beneficium* and *casamentum*, came to be used to describe a form of property holding. The holdings these terms denoted have often been considered essentially dependent tenures, over which their holders' rights were notably limited. As the words were used in documents of the period, however, the characteristics of the holdings to which they were applied are difficult to distinguish from those of tenures designated by such

Allodium

The medieval concept of allodium refers to land freely held, without obligation of service to any overlord. Allodial land tenure was of particular significance in western Europe during the Middle Ages, when most land was held by feudal tenure.

At the end of the 9th century the extent of allodial land in France was increased by the anarchy that accompanied the

(continued on the next page)

decline of the Carolingian monarchy; much of this new property, however, was eventually brought into a feudal relationship in which the holder owed certain services to his lord. By the 12th and 13th centuries, the only appreciable amount of allodial land remaining was limited to peasant holdings in the southwest. In Germany large allodial estates held by nobles continued to exist, particularly in Saxony. In England there was a considerable amount of allodial land before the Norman Conquest (1066), but it disappeared under the new rulers. Allodial land, though free of limitations from above, was not free of restrictions from below if the holder chose to have feudal tenants. He would then owe certain obligations to them, primarily in terms of protection, and could not be considered in absolute control of his holdings.

With the decline of feudalism in France, land that had been under the jurisdiction of a lord came to be under the jurisdiction of the king, who collected certain fees upon its sale or transfer. Following the French Revolution (1789) all land became allodial. In England no land is referred to as allodial, but an estate in fee simple corresponds in practice to absolute ownership.

words as "allodium," which has generally been translated as "freehold property."

Fiefs still existed in the 17th century, when the feudal model—or, as contemporary historians term it, the feudal construct—was developed. At that time, the fief was a piece of property, usually land, that was held in return for service, which could include military duties. The fief holder swore fidelity to the person from whom the fief was held (the lord, *dominus*, or seigneur) and became his (or her) man. The ceremony in which the oath was taken was called homage (from the Latin, *homo*; "man").

Detail from the Heidelberger Sachsenspiegel *showing the homage ceremony, in which the vassals put themselves under the protection of their lords by placing their hands between his hands, 14th century.* Universitatsbibliothek, Heidelberg, Germany

Charles II, detail of a painting by Sir Peter Lely, c. 1675; in the collection of the Duke of Grafton. Courtesy of the Duke of Grafton and the Royal Academy of Arts

These institutions survived in England until they were abolished by Parliament in 1645 and, after the Restoration, by Charles II in 1660. Until their eradication by the National Assembly between 1789 and 1793, they had considerable importance in France, where they were employed to create and reinforce familial and social bonds. Their pervasiveness made students of the past eager to understand how they had come into being. Similarities of terminology and practice found in documents surviving from the Middle Ages—especially the *Libri feudorum* ("Book of Fiefs"), an Italian compilation of customs relating to property holding, which was made in the 12th century and incorporated into Roman law—led historians and lawyers to search for the origins of contemporary feudal institutions in the Middle Ages.

Historians' Understanding of Feudalism

The characteristics of the feudal construct were in part deduced from medieval documents and chronicles, but they were interpreted in light of 17th-century practices and semantics. Learned legal commentaries on the laws governing the property called "fiefs" also affected interpretation of the sources. These commentaries, produced since the 13th century, focused on legal theory and on rules derived from actual disputes and hypothetical cases. They did not include (nor were they intended to provide) dispassionate analysis of historical development. Legal commentators in the 16th century had prepared the way for the elaboration of the feudal construct by formulating the idea, loosely derived from the *Libri feudorum*, of a single feudal law, which they presented as being spread throughout Europe during the early Middle Ages.

Characteristics of the Feudal System

As defined by scholars in the 17th century, the medieval feudal system was characterized by the absence of public authority and the exercise by local lords of administrative and judicial functions formerly (and later) performed by centralized governments; general disorder and endemic conflict; and the prevalence of bonds between lords and free dependents (vassals), which were forged by the lords' bestowal of property called fiefs and by their reception of homage from the vassals. These bonds entailed the rendering of services by vassals to their lords (military obligations, counsel, financial support) and the lords' obligation to protect and respect their vassals.

Vassal

In feudal society, a vassal was one invested with a fief in return for services to an overlord. Some vassals did not have fiefs and lived at their lord's court as his household knights. Certain vassals who held their fiefs directly from the crown were tenants in chief and formed the most important feudal group, the barons. A fief held by tenants of these tenants in chief was called an *arriere-fief*, and, when the king summoned the whole feudal host, he was said to summon the *ban et arriere-ban*. There were female vassals as well; their husbands fulfilled their wives' services.

Under the feudal contract, the lord had the duty to provide the fief for his vassal, to protect him, and to do him justice in his court. In return, the lord had the right to demand the services attached to the fief (military, judicial, administrative) and a right to various "incomes" known as feudal incidents. Examples of incidents are relief, a tax paid when a fief was transferred to an heir or alienated by the vassal, and scutage, a tax paid in lieu of military service. Arbitrary arrangements were gradually replaced by a system of fixed dues on occasions limited by custom.

The vassal owed fealty to his lord. A breach of this duty was a felony, regarded as so heinous an offense that in England all serious crimes, even those that had nothing to do with feudalism proper, came to be called felonies, since, in a way, they were breaches of the fealty owed to the king as guardian of the public peace and order.

Feudal Land Tenure

In medieval England and France, feudal land tenure was a system by which land was held by tenants from lords. The king was lord paramount, with numerous levels of lesser lords down to the occupying tenant.

Tenures were divided into free and unfree. Of the free tenures, the first was tenure in chivalry, principally grand sergeanty and knight service. The former obliged the tenant to perform some honourable and often personal service; knight service entailed performing military duties for the king or other lord, though by the middle of the 12th century such service was usually commuted for a payment called scutage. Another type of free tenure was socage, primarily customary socage, the principal service of which was usually agricultural in nature, such as performing so many days' plowing each year for the lord.

In addition to the principal service, all these tenures were subject to a number of conditions, such as relief, which was the payment made on transfer of a fief to an heir, and escheat, meaning the return of the fief to the lord when the vassal died without an heir. Chivalric tenures were also subject to wardship, which entailed the guardianship of a fief of a minor, and marriage; payment was made in lieu of marriage of the vassal's daughter to the lord.

Another form of free tenure was the spiritual tenure of bishops or monasteries, their sole obligation being to pray for the souls of the grantor and his heirs. Some ecclesiastics also held temporal lands for which they performed the required services.

The main type of unfree tenancy was villenage, initially a modified form of servitude. Whereas the mark of free tenants was that their services were always predetermined, in unfree tenure they were not; the unfree tenant never knew what he might be called to do for his lord. Although at first the villein tenant held his land entirely at the will of the lord and might be ejected at any time, the royal courts later protected him to the extent that he held tenancy at the will of the lord and according to the custom of the manor, so that he could not be ejected in breach of existing customs. Moreover, an unfree tenant could not leave without his lord's approval. Tenure in villeinage in England then became known as copyhold tenure (abolished after 1925), in which the holder was personally free and paid rent in lieu of services.

Benefice

"Benefice" was a term used to describe a particular kind of land tenure that came into use in the 8th century in the kingdom of the Franks. A Frankish sovereign or lord, the seigneur, leased an estate to a freeman on easy terms in *beneficium* (Latin: "for the benefit [of the tenant]"), and this came to be called a *beneficium*, a benefice. The lease normally came to an end on the death of the seigneur or of the tenant, though holders of benefices often succeeded in turning them into hereditary holdings.

Although by the 12th century "benefice" was dying out as a term for feudal land tenure, it retained an important place in the law of the Western Church and later in that of the Church of England; it came to designate an ecclesiastical office to which the church attached the perpetual right of receiving income. In the early history of the church, all endowments were generally centralized under the administration of the bishop, and there was no endowment attached to a particular ecclesiastical office. By the 8th century, churches were being founded in villages by the seigneurs, usually laymen, who were allowed to appoint the priest. Parish churches thus fell into two groups, the earlier type founded and controlled by bishops and the later type under the control of the lay seigneurs. Both bishops and seigneurs began to treat each church and its endowments as property to be leased like any other part of their estates, and they appointed the priest by leasing to him as a piece of property the church and its endowment in return for his carrying out the spiritual duties and frequently the paying of some rent. The priest held the church for life, unless a term of years was specifically mentioned in the lease.

In the 12th century the procedure for granting ecclesiastical benefices was made to conform to the ideals of Pope Gregory VII (reigned 1073–85). A lay seigneur could not grant an ecclesiastical office directly to a priest or receive rent or payment for it. The lay seigneur became the patron of the church; he chose the priest but could not lease him the church or receive any rent for it. The church had to be leased or granted to the priest by the bishop. Once inducted or invested with the benefice, the priest held it for life or, if he resigned, until his resignation was accepted by the bishop. Otherwise he was bound to vacate the benefice only if he was deprived of it in a court of law or if he received another benefice, in which case he automatically vacated the first benefice unless he had a dispensation to hold two or more benefices in plurality.

The procedure in the Church of England for giving a benefice to a priest and the terms on which he holds it have been modified in two respects. First, the bishop has wider powers of refusing the patron's nominee, and in a vacancy the parochial church council has the right to be consulted before an appointment is made. Second, the circumstances under which a priest can be removed from his benefice have been enlarged. In the Roman Catholic Church, the law concerning benefices has been set down in great detail in the Code of Canon Law (*Codex Juris Canonici*).

The benefice system, by making the parish priest dependent on no man's pleasure for his income or continuance in office, gave him an immeasurable status and strength in carrying out his duties.

Serfdom

Serfdom was a condition in medieval Europe in which a tenant farmer was bound to a hereditary plot of land and to the will of his landlord. The vast majority of serfs in medieval Europe obtained their subsistence by cultivating a plot of land that was owned by a lord. This was the essential feature differentiating serfs from slaves, who were bought and sold without reference to a plot of land. The serf provided his own food and clothing from his own productive efforts. A substantial proportion of the grain the serf grew on his holding had to be given to his lord. The lord could also compel the serf to cultivate that portion of the lord's land that was not held by other tenants (called demesne land). The serf also had to use his lord's grain mills and no others.

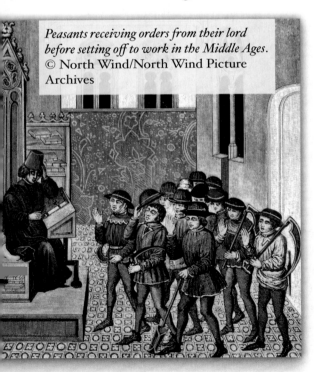

Peasants receiving orders from their lord before setting off to work in the Middle Ages. © North Wind/North Wind Picture Archives

The essential additional mark of serfdom was the lack of many of the personal liberties that were held by freedmen. Chief among these was the serf's lack of freedom of movement; he could not permanently leave his holding or his village without his lord's permission. Neither could the serf marry, change his occupation, or dispose of his property without his lord's permission. He was bound to his designated plot of land and could be transferred along with that land to a new lord. Serfs were often harshly treated and had little legal redress against the actions of their lords. A serf could become a freedman only through manumission, enfranchisement, or escape.

Serfs in the Roman Empire

From as early as the 2nd century CE, many of the large, privately held estates in the Roman Empire that had been worked by gangs of slaves were gradually broken up into peasant holdings. These peasants of the late Roman Empire, many of whom were descendants of slaves, came to depend on larger landowners and other important persons for protection from state tax collectors and, later, from barbarian invaders and oppressive neighbours. Some of these *coloni*, as the dependent peasants were called, may have taken up holdings granted them by a proprietor, or they may have surrendered their own lands to him in return for such protection. In any case, it became a practice for the dependent peasant to swear fealty to a proprietor, thus becoming bound to that lord.

The main problem with the *coloni* was that of preventing them from leaving the land they had agreed to cultivate as tenant farmers. The solution was to legally bind them to their holdings. Accordingly, a legal code established by the Roman emperor Constantine in 332 demanded labour services to be paid to the lord by the *coloni*. Although the *coloni* were legally free, the conditions of fealty required them to cultivate their lord's untenanted lands as well as their leased plot. This not only tied them to their holdings but also made their social status essentially servile, since the exaction of labour services required the landlord's agents to exercise discipline over the *coloni*. The threat, or the exercise, of this discipline was recognized as one of the clearest signs of a man's personal subjection.

By the 6th century the *servi*, or serfs, as the servile peasants came to be called, were treated as an inferior element in society. Serfs subsequently became a major class in the small, decentralized polities that characterized most of Europe from the fall of the Roman Empire in the 5th century to the initial reconstitution of feudal monarchies, duchies, and counties in the 12th century.

Manorialism

The term "feudalism" has been used most broadly to refer to medieval society as a whole, and in this way may be understood as a socioeconomic system that is often called manorialism. However, several scholars have differentiated between "feudalism" and "manorialism" by remarking that the former term referred to a political system, while the latter was primarily economic in nature.

Like feudalism, manorialism was a system wherein the peasants of medieval Europe were rendered dependent on their land and on their lord. Its basic unit was the manor, a self-sufficient landed estate, or fief, that was under the control of a lord who enjoyed a variety of rights over it and the peasants attached to it by means of serfdom. The manorial system was the most convenient device for organizing the estates of the aristocracy and the clergy in the European Middle Ages, and it made feudalism possible.

The Origins of Manorialism

Under other names (for instance, seignorialism), the manorial system was found not only in France, England, Germany, Italy, and Spain but also in varying degrees in the Byzantine Empire, Russia, Japan, and elsewhere. The manorial system's importance as an institution varied in different parts of

Europe at different times. In western Europe it was flourishing by the 8th century and had begun to decline by the 13th century, while in eastern Europe it achieved its greatest strength after the 15th century.

Manorialism had its origins in the late Roman Empire, when large landowners had to consolidate their hold over both their lands and the labourers who worked them. This was a necessity in the midst of the civil disorders, enfeebled governments, and barbarian invasions that wracked Europe in the 5th and 6th centuries CE. In such conditions, small farmers and landless labourers exchanged their land or their freedom and pledged their services in return for the protection of powerful landowners who had the military strength to defend them. In this way, the poor, defenseless, and landless were ensured permanent access to plots of land which they could work in return for the rendering of economic services to the lord who held that land. This arrangement developed into the manorial system, which in turn supported the feudal aristocracy of kings, lords, and vassals.

Lay of the Medieval Land

The typical western European manor in the 13th century consisted partly of the cottages, huts, and barns and gardens of its peasants, which were usually clustered together to form a small village. The village itself was surrounded by arable land that was divided into three large fields that were farmed in rotation, with one allowed to lie fallow each year. There were also usually meadows for supplying hay, pastures for livestock, pools and streams for fishing, and forests and wastelands for wood gathering and foraging.

The lord would grant part of his land out to free tenants to hold at a rent or by military or other service. Below the lord and the free tenants came the villeins, serfs, or bondmen, each holding a hut or small dwelling, a fixed number of acre strips, and a share of the meadow and of the profits of the waste. Most of the forest and wastelands, and a portion of the cultivated land, were held by the lord as his demesne, i.e., that portion of a manor not granted to free tenants but either retained by the lord for his own use and occupation or occupied by his villeins or leasehold tenants.

Under the manorialism system, villeins normally were unfree; they could not quit the manor without leave of the lord and could be reclaimed by process of law if they did. The strict contention of law deprived them of all right to hold property. In many cases, they were subject to certain degrading incidents, such as *marchet* (*merchetum*), a payment due to the lord upon the marriage of a daughter, which was regarded as a special mark of unfree condition.

But there were certain limitations. First, all these incidents of tenure, even *marchet*, might not affect the personal status of the tenant; he might still be free, though held by an unfree tenure. Second, even if unfree, he was not exposed to the arbitrary will of his lord but was protected by the custom of the manor as interpreted by the manor court. Moreover, he was not a slave, since he could not be bought and sold apart from his holding. Instead, the hardship of his condition lay in the services due from him.

As a rule a villein paid for his holding in money, labour, and agrarian produce. In money he paid, first, a small fixed rent that was known as rent of assize and, second, dues under various names, partly in lieu of services commuted into money payments and partly for the privileges and profits enjoyed by him on the waste of the manor. In labour he paid more heavily. Week by week he was required to come with his own plow and oxen to plow the lord's demesne; when plowing was completed, he had to harrow, to reap the crops, to thresh and carry them, or to do whatever might be required of him, until his allotted number of days' labour in the year had been accomplished.

The Manor House

Establishments inside the manorial village might include a church, a mill, and a wine or oil press. Close by was the fortified dwelling, or manor house. During the European Middle Ages, the manor house was the dwelling of the lord of the manor or his residential bailiff and administrative centre of the feudal estate. The medieval manor was generally fortified in proportion to the degree of peaceful settlement of the country or region in which it was located. The manor house was the centre of secular village life, and its great hall was the scene of the manorial court and the place of assembly of

Reenactors demonstrate a medieval dance in England's Great Hall at Eltham Palace. A manor's hall served as a gathering spot for meals, entertainment, and other purposes. Oli Scarff/Getty Images

the tenantry. The hall was the main apartment in a medieval manor house in which meals were taken. In large manor houses it also served other purposes: justice was administered there, entertainments given, and often at night the floor was strewn with rushes so that many of the servants could sleep there.

The particular character of the manor house is most clearly represented in England and France, but under different names similar dwellings of feudal overlords existed in all countries wherein the manorial system developed. In England in the 11th century the manor house was an informal group of related timber or stone buildings consisting of the hall, chapel, kitchen, and farm buildings contained within a defensive wall and ditch. In the 12th century the hall, which throughout the medieval period was the major element of domestic architecture, was placed defensively at first-floor level and contained within a moated enclosure. Later it was planned at ground level, as in Oakham Castle, Rutland, within a more strongly defended enclosure.

By the 14th century the manor-house plan was clearly defined, with private living apartments and service rooms at opposite ends of the great hall and with battlements, gatehouse, and moat—as at Ightham Mote, Kent. Ockwells Manor in Berkshire is a typical timber-framed manor house built in the 15th century without defensive elements.

In France, until the end of the Hundred Years' War in 1453, considerations of defense dominated manorial building. Such early manor houses as the 14th-century Camarsac Manor in Gironde consisted primarily of a rectangular fortified tower in a walled and moated enclosure. In Normandy the Ango Manor, near Dieppe, reveals some advance in domestic planning in the 15th century, the house standing at one end of a courtyard, flanked by farm buildings and defended by a gatehouse.

Gatehouse of the manor house at Ightham Mote, Kent, Eng. A.F. Kersting

With increased prosperity and the desire for more commodious dwellings, the 16th-century manor house evolved into the Renaissance country house. In England more elaborate buildings were constructed, reflecting a new era of formality. The houses were frequently of regular quadrangular plan, with the hall diminished in size and importance. Later the hall was reduced to the status of an entrance, as at Ramsbury Manor, Wiltshire (c. 1680). The defended tower-house tradition persisted in France throughout the 16th century, generally retaining corner turrets and other defensive archaisms, as in the Tourelles Manor, near Troyes.

In later years the title of manor house in England lost particular significance, having been adopted by large country mansions that had no manorial foundation which might be inhabited by him or merely by his steward if the lord happened to hold more than one manor.

The Manor Court

The most complicated structure in the system was the manor court, whose business was divided into criminal, manorial, and civil. Under feudal law, this was the court through which a lord exercised jurisdiction over his tenants. The manorial court was presided over by the steward or seneschal, and it was there that various officials—such as the reeve, who acted as general overseer, and the hayward, who watched over the crops and brought offenders to court—were appointed. Tenants were punished and often forced to pay fines for their offenses; the manorial court thus provided the lord with a convenient source of income. Through the court, tenants also registered land transactions between themselves—when this was permitted—and surrendered or took up holdings under the lord. Manorial courts declined in the 17th century and were generally obsolete in the 18th century.

Its powers under the first head depended on the franchises enjoyed by the lord in the particular manor; for the most part only petty offenses were triable, such as small thefts, breaches of the assize of bread and ale, assaults, and the like; except under special conditions, the justice of great offenses remained in the hands of the king or other territorial sovereign. But offenses against the custom of the manor, such as bad plowing, improper taking of wood from the lord's woods, and the like were of course the staple criminal business of the court. Under the head of manorial business, the court dealt with the choice of the manorial officers and had some power of making regulations for the management of the manor; but its most important function was the recording of the surrenders and admittances of the villein tenants. Finally, the court dealt with all suits as to land within the manor, questions of dower and inheritance, and those few civil suits not connected with land.

The revival of commerce that began in Europe in the 11th century signaled the decline of the manorial system, which could only survive in a decentralized and localized economy in which peasant subsistence farming was dominant. The reintroduction of a money economy into Europe and the growth of cities and towns in the 11th and 12th centuries created a market for the lords' agricultural produce and also provided luxuries for them to purchase. As a result, lords increasingly allowed their peasants to commute their (labour) services for money and eventually to purchase their freedom with it as well. Agricultural surpluses could now be sold to the cities and towns, and it was found that free workers who paid rent or received wages farmed more efficiently (and produced more profits) than enserfed labourers. Owing to these and other economic reasons, the inefficient and coercive manorial system disintegrated in western Europe, gradually evolving into simpler and less onerous economic arrangements between landlords and rent-paying tenants.

Manorialism underwent a somewhat different evolution in central and eastern Europe. These areas had witnessed the decline of manorialism in the 12th and 13th centuries as vast areas of forest and wasteland were colonized by free German and Slavonic peasants. But the numerous wars fought between the Russians, Poles, Prussians, Lithuanians, and others in the 15th and 16th centuries reproduced the political instability and social insecurities that had led to peasant enserfment in western Europe centuries earlier. In addition, western Europe's growing demand for grain from the Baltic area gave nobles and other landlords there an additional incentive to enserf their peasants, since that was the best way to ensure labour services for grain-growing demesnes. So by the 16th century manorialism had been re-created on a large scale in eastern Europe, particularly in eastern Germany, Poland, and Russia. These reactionary manorial developments were not reversed in eastern Europe until the 19th century in most cases.

European Feudalism in Perspective

The terms "feudalism" and "feudal system" enabled historians to deal summarily with a long span of European history whose complexities were—and remain—confusing. The Roman Empire and the various emperors' accomplishments provided a key to understanding Roman history, and the reemergence of states and strong rulers in the 12th century again furnished manageable focal points for historical narrative, particularly since medieval states and governmental practices can be presented as antecedents of modern nations and institutions. The feudal construct neatly filled the gap between the 5th and the 12th century.

Although Charlemagne may seem an anomaly in this evolution, he was presented as "sowing the seeds" from which feudalism emerged. A variety of Roman, barbarian, and Carolingian institutions were considered antecedents of feudal practices: Roman lordship and clientage, barbarian war chiefdoms and bands, grants of lands to soldiers and to officeholders, and oaths of loyalty and fidelity.

In the 17th century, as later, the high point of feudalism was located in the 11th century. Later rulers who adopted and adapted feudal institutions to increase their power were labeled "feudal" and their governments called "feudal monarchies." Despite the survival of institutions and practices associated with the medieval feudal system in the 17th century, historians of that time presented medieval feudalism and the feudal system as declining in importance in the 14th and 15th centuries. This period was later dubbed an age of "bastard feudalism" because of the use of salaries and written contracts between lords and dependents.

CHAPTER 2

THE NATURE OF MONARCHIES

A monarchy is a political system based upon the undivided sovereignty or rule of a single person. The term applies to states in which supreme authority is vested in the monarch, an individual ruler who functions as the head of state and who achieves his position through heredity. Succession usually passes from father to son or follows other arrangements within the family or the monarchical dynasty.

Functions of Monarchies

A monarchy consists of distinct but interdependent institutions—a government and a state administration on the one hand, and a court and a variety of ceremonies on the other—that provide for the social life of the members of the dynasty, their friends, and the associated elite. Monarchy thus entails not only a political-administrative organization but also a "court society," a term coined by the 20th-century German-born sociologist Norbert Elias to designate various groups of nobility that are linked to the monarchical dynasty (or "royal" house) through a web of personal bonds. All such bonds are evident in symbolic and ceremonial proprieties.

During a given society's history there are certain changes and processes that create conditions conducive to the rise of monarchy. Because warfare was the main means of acquiring fertile land and trade routes, some of the most prominent monarchs in the ancient world made their initial mark as warrior-leaders. Thus, the military accomplishments of Octavian (later Augustus) led to his position as emperor and to the institution of monarchy in the Roman Empire. Infrastructural programs and state-building also contributed to the development of monarchies. The need, common in arid cultures, to allocate fertile land and manage a regime of fresh water distribution (what the German-American historian Karl Wittfogel called hydraulic civilization) accounted for the founding of the ancient Chinese, Egyptian, and Babylonian monarchies on the banks of rivers. The monarchs also had to prove themselves as state-builders.

Monarchy also results from the wish of a society—be it a city population, tribe, or multi-tribal "people"—to groom an indigenous leader who will properly represent its historical goals and advance its interests. Monarchy, therefore, rests on the cultural identity and symbolism of the society it represents, and in so doing it reifies that identity within the society while also projecting it to outsiders. Perhaps most importantly, successful and popular monarchs were believed to have a sacred right to rule. Some were regarded as gods (as in the case of the Egyptian pharaohs or the Japanese monarchs), some were crowned by priests, others were designated by prophets (King David of Israel), and still others were

Image depicting the coronation of Charlemagne by Pope Leo III, thus confirming the emperor's divine right to rule in the eyes of the empire's subjects.
Apic/Hulton Archive/Getty Images

theocrats, leading both the religious and political spheres of their society—as did the caliphs of the Islamic state from the 7th century CE.

Coming from these varying backgrounds, leaders first rose to power on the grounds of their abilities and charisma. Accordingly, monarchies proved capable of adapting to various social structures while also enduring dynamic cultural and geopolitical conditions. Thus, some ancient monarchies evolved as small city-states while others became large empires, the Roman Empire being the most conspicuous example.

Premodern Monarchies

During the Middle Ages, European monarchies underwent a process of evolution and transformation. Tradi-

Gregory VII laying a ban of excommunication on the clergy loyal to Germany's King Henry IV; drawing from the 12th-century chronicle of Otto von Freising. Leonard von Matt/ EB Inc.

tions of theocratic kingship, which were based on Roman and Christian precedents, emerged in the early centuries of the period, leading kings to assume their status as God's representatives on earth. Early medieval monarchs functioned as rulers of their people (rather than as territorial lords), and each was responsible for their people's protection. In the 11th century, however, the Gregorian Reform, and the Investiture Controversy associated with it, undermined the claims of theocratic kingship, and monarchs—most notably the emperors—looked to Roman law for new justification of their right to rule.

Throughout the Middle Ages, kings had come to power through conquest, acclamation, election, or inheritance. Medieval monarchs ruled through their courts, which were at first private households but from the 12th century developed into more formal and institutional bureaucratic structures. It was during the 12th century as well that kings evolved into rulers of people and of territories with defined borders. By the end of the Middle Ages, the development of the territorial monarchies had laid the foundation for the idea of the modern nation-state.

Medieval Monarchies Outside Europe

Unlike in Europe, the Islamic monarchy, the caliphate, remained unified and theocratic, combining religious and lay functions. In Japan, the monarchy conceded real power to the shogunate, which was technically controlled by the emperor but in practice dominated by the shogun, a supreme warlord. Attempts to attain this position often resulted in interdynastic conflict. In China, the monarchy evolved as a centralized bureaucratic body, held by a succession of various dynasties.

From Territorial Principalities to Territorial Monarchies

As a result of the Investiture Controversy of the late 11th and early 12th centuries, the office of emperor lost much of its religious character and retained only a nominal universal preeminence over other rulers, though several 12th- and 13th-century emperors reasserted their authority on the basis of their interpretation of Roman law and energetically applied their lordship and pursued their dynastic interests in Germany and northern Italy. But the struggle over investiture and the reform movement also legitimized all secular authorities, partly on the grounds of their obligation to enforce discipline. The most successful rulers of the 12th and 13th centuries were, first, individual lords who created compact and more intensely governed principalities and, second and most important and enduring, kings who successfully asserted their authority over the princes, often with princely cooperation. The monarchies of England, France, León-Castile, Aragon, Scandinavia, Portugal, and elsewhere all acquired their fundamental shape and character in the 12th century.

The Office and Person of the King

By the 12th century, most European political thinkers agreed that monarchy was the ideal form of governance, since it imitated on earth the model set by God for the universe. It was also the form of government of the ancient Hebrews, the Roman Empire, and the peoples who succeeded Rome after the 4th century. For several centuries, some areas had no monarch, but these were regarded as anomalies. Iceland (until its absorption by Norway in 1262) was governed by an association of free men and heads of households meeting in an annual assembly. Many city-republics in northern Italy—especially Florence, Milan, Genoa, Pisa, and Venice—were in effect independent from the 10th to the 16th century, though they were nominally under the rule of the emperor. Elsewhere in Europe, the prosperous and volatile cities of the Low Countries frequently asserted considerable independence from the counts of Flanders and the dukes of Brabant. In the 15th century the forest cantons of Switzerland won effective independence from their episcopal and lay masters. For the rest of Europe, however, monarchy was both a theoretical norm and a factual reality.

Whereas kings were originally rulers of peoples, from the 11th century they gradually became rulers of peoples in geographic territories, and kingdoms came to designate both ruled peoples and the lands they inhabited. Gradually, inventories of royal resources, royal legislation, and the idea of borders and territorial maps became components of territorial monarchies.

Kings acquired their thrones by inheritance, by election or acclamation (as in the empire), or by conquest. The first two means were considered the most legitimate, unless conquest was carried out at the request or command of a legitimate authority, usually the pope. The king's position was confirmed by a coronation ceremony, which acknowledged what royal blood claimed: a dynastic right to the throne, borne by a family rather than a designated individual. Inheritance of the throne might involve the successor's being designated coruler while the previous king still lived (as in France), designation by the will of the predecessor, or simply agreement and acclamation by the most important and powerful royal subjects. When dynasties died out in the male line, the search for a ruler became more complicated; when they died out in the male line and a woman succeeded, there were usually intense debates about the legitimacy of female succession. Liturgical anointing with consecrated oil was accompanied by the ceremonial presentation to the king of objects with symbolic meaning (the crown, the sword of justice, and the helmet, robe, and scepter), by the chanting of prayers dedicated to rulership, and usually by an oath, in which the king swore to protect the church, the weak, and the peace of his kingdom, to administer justice, and to defend the kingdom against its (and his) enemies.

From the very beginning of European history, kings had responsibilities as well as rights and powers. Kings who were thought to have violated their oaths might be considered tyrants or incompetents, and a number of kings were deposed by local factions or papal command, especially in the 13th and 14th centuries. Depositions also required ceremonies that reversed the coronation liturgy.

Instruments of Royal Governance

Kings ruled through their courts, which were gradually transformed from private households into elaborate bureaucracies. Royal religious needs were served by royal chapels—whose personnel often became bishops in the kingdom—and by clerical chancellors, who were responsible for issuing and sealing royal documents. Royal chanceries, financial offices, and law courts became specialized institutions during the 12th century. They recruited people of skill as well as of respectable birth, and they established programs to ensure uniformity and norms of professional competence, goals that were increasingly aided by the education offered by the new universities.

In some circumstances, kings were expected to seek and follow the advice of the most important men in their kingdoms, and these gatherings were formalized after the 12th century. Kings also sometimes convened larger assemblies of lower-ranking subjects in order to issue their commands or urge approval of financial demands. As kings grew stronger and their bureaucracies more articulated, their costs, particularly for war, also increased. Greater financial needs often determined a king's use of representative institutions in order to gain widespread acceptance of new direct or indirect taxation.

These assemblies developed differently in different kingdoms. In England the first Parliaments were held in the late 13th century, though they were not powerful institutions until the 16th century. In France the Parlement developed into a royal law court, while the intermittent meetings of the Estates-General (a representative assembly of the three orders of society) served as an instrument of consultation and communication for the kings. Across Europe these representative assemblies were composed differently, functioned differently, and possessed different degrees of influence on the ruler and the rest of the kingdom. Their later role as essential and powerful components of government began only in the 16th and 17th centuries.

The territorial monarchies represented something entirely new in world history. Although they often borrowed from the political literature of antiquity——from the Greek philosopher Aristotle, the Roman statesman Cicero, and Roman epic poetry—they applied it to a very different world, one whose ideas were shaped by courtiers, professors, and canon lawyers as well as by political philosophers. Incorporating both clergy and laity under vigorous royal dynasties, the kingdoms of Europe grew out of the political experience of the papacy, the north Italian city-republics, and their own internal development. By the 15th century the territorial monarchies had laid the groundwork for the modern state. When, to further their own interests, they began to incorporate successively lower levels of society, they also laid the groundwork for the nation. The combination of these, the nation-state, became the characteristic form of the early modern European and Atlantic polity.

The Three Orders

In the 11th and 12th centuries thinkers argued that human society consisted of three orders: those who fight, those who pray, and those who labour. The structure of the second order, the clergy, was in place by 1200 and remained intact until the religious reformations of the 16th century. The very general category of those who labour (specifically, those who were not knightly warriors or nobles) diversified rapidly after the 11th century into the lively and energetic worlds of peasants, skilled artisans, merchants, financiers, lay professionals, and entrepreneurs, which together drove the European economy to its greatest achievements. The first order, those who fight, was the rank of the politically powerful, ambitious, and dangerous. Kings took pains to ensure that it did not resist their authority.

The term "noble" was originally used to refer to members of kinship groups whose names and heroic past were known, respected, and recognized by others (though it was not usually used by members of such groups themselves). Noble groups married into each other, recognizing the importance of both the female and the male lines. Charlemagne used this international nobility to rule his empire, and its descendants became the nobility of the 11th and 12th centuries, though by then the understanding of noble status had changed. During the 11th century, however, some branches of these broad groups began to identify themselves increasingly with the paternal line and based their identity on their possession of a particular territory handed down from generation to generation, forming patriarchal lineages whose consciousness of themselves differed from that of their predecessors. Titles such as count or duke were originally those of royal service and might increase the prestige and wealth of a family but were not originally essential to noble status. Nor were even kings thought to be able to ennoble someone who was not noble by birth. As the status of the free peasant population was diminished, freedom and unfreedom, as noted above, gradually became the most significant social division.

The new warrior order encompassed both great nobles and lesser fighting men who depended upon the great nobles for support. This assistance usually took the form of land or income drawn from the lord's resources, which could also bring the hope of social advancement, even marriage into a lordly family. The acute need on the part of these lower-ranking warriors was to distinguish themselves from peasants—hence the relegation of all who were not warriors to the vague category of those who labour.

Some nobles asserted their nobility by seizing territory, controlling it and its inhabitants from a castle, surviving as

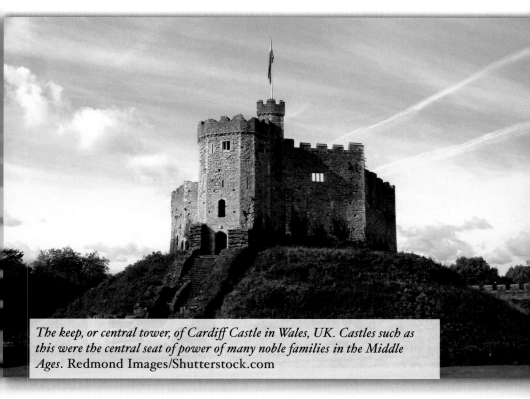

The keep, or central tower, of Cardiff Castle in Wales, UK. Castles such as this were the central seat of power of many noble families in the Middle Ages. Redmond Images/Shutterstock.com

local powers over several generations, marrying well, achieving recognition from their neighbours, and dispensing ecclesiastical patronage to nearby monasteries. The greatest and wealthiest of the nobles controlled vast areas of land, which they received by inheritance or through a grant from the king. Some of them developed closely governed territorial principalities which, in France, were eventually absorbed and redistributed by the crown to members of the royal family or their favourites. Despite the extreme diversity between knights, lesser nobility, and greater nobility, their common warrior-culture, expressed in the literature and ideology of chivalry, served as an effective social bond, excluding all those who did not share it.

As the territorial monarchies gradually increased in both prestige and power, the higher nobility adjusted by accepting more royal offices, titles, and patronage, developing an elaborate vocabulary of noble status, and restricting access to its ranks even though kings could now ennoble whomever they chose. The culture of chivalry served the ambitions of the lower-ranking nobility, but it also reflected the spectrum of different levels of nobility, all subordinated to the ruler. The culture and power of the European aristocracy lasted until the end of the 18th century.

Early Post-Feudal European Monarchies

The Renaissance and early modern period led to a newly adapted type of monarchy in Europe, with monarchs initiating voyages of discovery to other continents, developing new forms of mercantile trade, and, most of all, building mass armies and large government bureaucracies that represented innovative forms of political administration. Compared to their predecessors, the monarchs of this era were better able to monitor and manage their own societies, to exact more taxes, and to decide on interstate war and conquest. The Renaissance monarchs, such as Charles V (reigned 1519–56), Francis I (1515–47), and Elizabeth I (1558–1603), unified their realms and strengthened their bureaucracies. However, later monarchs, such as Catherine the Great of Russia (reigned 1762–96), Louis XIV of France (1643–1715), and Frederick the Great of Prussia (1740–86), symbolized "absolutist" rule, as exemplified by Louis XIV's declaration, "L'état, c'est moi" ("I am the state"). Possessing complete administrative and military power, an absolute monarch could bypass the feudal lords or subjugate independent city-states and run his kingdom with individual autonomy or arbitrariness.

Yet in most cases absolute monarchy was absolutist only in appearance. In practice, most monarchs remained dependent upon chosen administrators to whom they had delegated the

Queen Elizabeth I presiding over Parliament; engraving, 1608. Print Collector/Hulton Archive/ Getty Images

authority to govern their states, as was the case in France. These officials were checked by institutions such as Great Britain's Parliament, or balanced by factions of the landed aristocracy, as in Russia and Poland. Monarchs were thus able to exploit their power, adding onto their traditional legitimacies while allowing for certain checks on their regimes, all of which seemed to portend continuous stability, had changes in the prevailing social and economic order not challenged the future of absolutist monarchies. One force of change, the Reformation (and the factionalism associated with it), triggered protracted religious conflicts, while the Industrial Revolution unleashed social unrest and class conflict—all of which occurred amid ongoing developments in international trade, investments, and other complex financial transactions that provoked economic problems such as inflation.

Most important, new perceptions emerged, first in Europe and then in the Middle East, Asia, and Africa, that reduced the monarchs' authority. The concept of "divine right" was often eroded by the spread of secularism. Emerging ideas of the individual's natural rights (as espoused by the philosophers John Locke and Jean-Jacques Rousseau and further evidenced by the Declaration of Independence of the United States) and those of nations' rights (particularly regarding independence and self-determination) gained prominence. Moreover, the monarchs' traditional supremacy, anchored in their lineage as descendants of war heroes and of leading notables, gradually weakened in favour of what the German-born American sociologist Reinhard Bendix called "a mandate of the people." Thus, a society's "sovereignty," or its principles of independence, cohesion, and leadership, rested with its people as a whole and not with an individual and his dynasty.

Monarchies were therefore challenged by various opposition movements. Although the British monarchy was able to cope with religious strife as well as social unrest among the rural and urban lower classes, the monarchies in France (beginning in 1789), Russia (1917), and China (1911) were swept away by popular social revolutions. The Austrian, German, and Ottoman monarchies also collapsed after World War I, having been defeated militarily and replaced by indigenous nationalist movements. It then became evident that monarchies could survive only if they were built upon a foundation of broad, nationalist-popular support, benefiting from a majority coalition of social forces.

Monarchy in the Modern Era

When he crowned himself emperor of France in 1804 (and ratified the act by a people's referendum), Napoleon Bonaparte instituted a new type of monarchy. This was the "nationalist monarchy," whereby the monarch ruled on behalf of his society's nationalist aspirations and drive for independence (as opposed to the earlier types of legitimacy). Napoleon based his rule on the instruments of the French Revolution, such as the Declaration of the Rights of Man and of the Citizen. He was also, however, an absolutist monarch who installed his family members as rulers in several European states that had fallen under his control.

Having taken root in Europe, nationalist monarchies spread to other parts of the world. In the 19th and early 20th centuries, new monarchs came to power in Greece and the Arab provinces (notably Egypt and Syria) and in states that had gained independence from the Ottoman Empire and the Austro-Hungarian Empire. The monarchs of this era wished to emphasize the modern identity of their nations, and in so doing they attempted to use their imperial titles as proof of modernity, even as they aspired to achieve equal footing with established, prominent monarchs such as the British royalty.

Their ultimate political influence, however, was limited: under their leadership political institutions failed to root themselves in society, and economies remained relatively underdeveloped. Unable to meet the needs of mass societies, the nationalist monarchs could not withstand the waves of major opposition movements, typical of the mid-20th century, which were either anticolonial, nationalist, or Marxist. These movements regarded all monarchies as bastions of an old, obsolete order that had to be eradicated. Monarchs were blamed for social injustice, political corruption, and economic backwardness, and they were consequently overthrown. Monarchies had acquired an image of a defeated, outdated system.

This mainly typified the absolutist monarchies led by rulers who exercised full authority as heads of states. In the midst of this, however, emerged a group of European monarchies that adapted to the new challenges. These became the "constitutional monarchies," the leading contemporary examples of which are the United Kingdom, Belgium, the Netherlands, Norway, Sweden, and Denmark. In these states, a legacy of political bargaining has existed, witnessing the monarch's gradual transfer of authority to various societal groups. Although the monarch remains the head of state and the emblem of state authority, the sovereign accepts that this authority has been transposed to that of a formal position, and the monarch waives actual political power, which is assumed by the people. In such monarchies political authority is exercised by elected politicians, and the political process runs according to democratic procedures. Hence, the monarch functions as a unifying and symbolic head of state who performs ceremonial duties, while the monarchical traditions and ceremonies have become national assets that symbolize historical continuity.

Monarchical Systems

Although the institution of monarchy is as old as recorded history, since the beginning of the modern era many monarchies have been replaced with republics. Of the monarchies that remain—such as those in the United Kingdom, Japan, Spain, the Scandinavian countries, and the Low Countries—many are best described as "constitutional monarchies," wherein the monarchs are primarily titular heads of state and do not in fact possess important powers of government. Most of the executive powers are in the hands of ministers—headed by a prime minister—who are politically responsible to the parliament and not to the monarch. The executive powers of government in the United Kingdom, for example, are exercised by ministers who hold their offices by virtue of the fact that they command the support of a majority in the popularly elected House of Commons. A constitutional monarch can act only on the advice of the ministers. The position of the monarchs in Scandinavia and the Low Countries is similar to that of the monarch in Britain: they reign but do not rule.

In countries where no political party has a majority of its own in the parliament, the monarch may exercise some discretion in deciding whom to invite to form a government. Even where they have this discretion, however, monarchs must first consult with the various party leaders, a requirement that severely limits their freedom of action. In countries with stable two-party systems, all the monarch can do is offer the prime ministership to the leader of the majority party. Since 1975 the Swedish king has not even possessed this formal power; it is the president of the legislative assembly who chooses and appoints the prime minister. A constitutional monarch is the head of the state, not of the government. Standing above the political controversies of the moment, the sovereign is an object of national pride and loyalty and a symbol of the nation's unity and its continuity with the past.

In a few monarchies, however—for example, those of Jordan, Morocco, and Saudi Arabia—the king exercises real powers of government. The ministers are chosen by and are responsible only to the king rather than to an elective parliamentary body. Hereditary rulers with this degree of personal power were quite common in the 18th century but are rare today. Although Jordan and Morocco have augmented the powers of their elected parliaments, the monarchs retain ultimate authority in those countries. In Thailand the constitution promulgated in 1932 greatly reduced the powers of the monarch, relegating him to a role similar to that of the

Hereditary Succession

"The king is dead; long live the king" was the answer, not always uncontested, of European hereditary monarchy to the question of who should rule after the death of the king. Apart from a few states where the dynastic ruler is the effective head of the government, the hereditary principle of succession is now almost exclusively confined to the constitutional monarchies of western Europe.

Heredity may be reinforced or modified by constitutional prescription. This was the case, for example, of the famous Act of Settlement (1701) that secured the Hanoverian succession in Britain.

There is some irony in the fact that the line of succession is more securely established in these monarchies in the modern era than at any point in their earlier history. It appears that intradynastic struggle is much less likely when kingship is mainly ceremonial.

European monarchs. Although he retained considerable formal powers, he could exercise them only upon the advice of elected leaders. His most important function was to serve as a living symbol of the country and as a focus of national unity.

Traditional Monarchies of the Middle East

By the early 21st century, examples of traditional monarchies were largely limited to the Arab world. These included the six oil-rich states, located along the Persian Gulf—Kuwait, Saudi Arabia, Bahrain, Qatar, the United Arab Emirates, and Oman—as well as Jordan and Morocco. Their longevity can only partially be accounted for by the abundance of oil revenues that made it possible for their monarchs to overpower any opposition groups. Jordan and Morocco, after all, were not awash in oil wealth but were among the most stable regimes in the region. The fact that many of these states benefited from U.S. and British military support certainly accounts for some of their perseverance in the face of external threats, as was the case for Kuwait in 1960–61 and more overtly in the Persian Gulf War (1990–91).

The stability of Arab monarchies has rested largely upon their political and cultural underpinnings, where the idea of a single hereditary ruler—or, rather, a single hereditary ruling family—has maintained a high degree of social currency. In the case of the Persian Gulf states, local monarchies have thrived by grafting themselves to the existing tribal framework. Such a system differs significantly from the concept of monarchy found in other parts of the world inasmuch as power lies in the hands of a ruling family—an extended entity whose members can number in the thousands—rather than in the hands of a single individual. In that system, the king is merely the head of the ruling family, a situation that early European orientalists described by recycling the phrase *primus inter pares*. Just as the monarch is the first among equals (*primus inter pares*) in the ruling family, the ruling family itself is the first among equals among the tribes of a given country. In such a situation, the ruling family maintains its position by mollifying dissenting opinions, addressing grievances, distributing largesse, and, when necessary, squelching extreme views through the selective use of coercive power. (In Saudi Arabia, the monarchy also relies to a great extent on religious legitimacy.) Such political systems can be loosely described as pluralistic, since membership in any extended family group or tribe grants one a voice in ongoing events. Those outside the tribal system, however, often have little political voice.

The monarch and his family maintain political stability by managing events and by building political alliances. Stability is further advanced in the Persian Gulf monarchies by the fact that a significant portion of the population belongs to the royal family. Under rare circumstances, the royal family will dethrone a monarch if his inattention or incompetence threaten the family's place at the head of society. Such an event occurred when Sa'ūd, king of Saudi Arabia, was dethroned in 1964.

The monarchies of Morocco and Jordan, both of which resemble traditional monarchies, have thrived for different reasons. In Morocco, the king is also a religious figure of great importance. In Jordan, the Hashemite monarchy owes its longevity to the exceptional political acumen of Hussein ibn Ṭalāl (reigned 1953–99), which secured political power for the family.

The ruling families of the gulf Arab states have proved themselves effective state-builders by introducing

Jordan's King 'Abdullah II. Thomas Koehler/Photothek/Getty Images

technological innovations and social modernity into their societies while enforcing a conservative political atmosphere. Such monarchies have proved to be effective integrators of their societies. They did not achieve this by enforcing a new, socialist, Arab-nationalist, and revolutionary character on society—as did revolutionary states such as Syria and Egypt. Instead they waived that pretension to create a uniform society and permitted socio-cultural variety, intended to befit traditional sentiments.

Monarchies in the 20th and 21st Centuries

The ancient distinction among monarchies, tyrannies, oligarchies, and constitutional governments, like other traditional classifications of political systems, is no longer very descriptive of political life. A king may be a ceremonial head of state, as in a parliamentary democracy, or he may be a head of government, perhaps even functioning as an absolute ruler. In the first case his duties may be little different from those of an elected president in many republican parliamentary regimes; in the second his role may be much the same as a dictator in an autocratic regime.

It may be said of the reigning dynasties of modern Europe that they have survived only because they failed to retain or to acquire effective powers of government. Royal lines have been preserved only in those countries of Europe in which royal rule was severely limited prior to the 20th century or in which royal absolutism had never firmly established itself. More successful dynasties, such as the Hohenzollerns in Germany, the Habsburgs in Austria-Hungary, and the Romanovs in Russia, which continued to rule as well as to reign at the opening of the 20th century, paid with the loss of their thrones. Today in countries such as Great Britain, the Netherlands, or Denmark, the monarch is the ceremonial head of state, an indispensable figure in all great official occasions and a symbol of national unity and of the authority of the state, but is almost entirely lacking in power. Monarchy in the parliamentary democracies of modern Europe has been reduced to the status of a dignified institutional facade behind which the functioning mechanisms of government—cabinet, parliament, ministries, and parties—go about the tasks of ruling.

The 20th century also saw the demise of most of the hereditary monarchies of the non-Western world. Thrones toppled in Turkey, in China, in most of the Arab countries, in the principates of India, in the tribal kingdoms of Africa, and in several countries of Southeast Asia. The kings who maintain their position do so less by the claim of legitimate blood descent than by their appeal as popular leaders responsible for well-publicized programs of national economic and social reform or as national military chieftains. In a sense, these kings are less monarchs than monocrats, and their regimes are little different from several other forms of one-man rule found in the modern world.

CHAPTER 3

NOBILITY AND THE RULING CLASS

Class distinctions are nearly as old as organized human society. They became established through the exercise of power and the accumulation of wealth by a few members of society. Distinctions between the few and the many were then perpetuated by inheritance and by law. In the ancient world the few were society's rulers: kings and nobles, priests, and the military leadership. The many were the mass of citizens who did most of society's work. There was no group between these two social segments comparable to today's middle class.

During the Middle Ages, European society gradually settled into a set of fairly rigid class relationships commonly known as feudalism. Kings owned the land, which they sectioned off into fiefs controlled by the nobles, thus creating a social class one step below royalty, but certainly above common peasants. The English word "nobility" comes from the Latin word *nobilitas*, which means "fame or celebrity." The term came to be applied to the class of land owners who were celebrities, in the sense of being special and privileged, of their day.

The Aristocracy

In its broadest interpretation, aristocracy refers to a government run by a relatively small privileged class or by a minority consisting of those felt to be best qualified to rule. As conceived by the Greek philosophers Plato (c. 428/427–348/347 BCE) and Aristotle (384–322 BCE), aristocracy means the rule of the few best—the morally and intellectually superior—governing in the interest of the entire population. Such a form of government differs from the rule of one (by a monarchy or by a tyrant); of the ambitious, self-interested, or greedy few (oligarchy or timocracy); or of the many (democracy or mobocracy). Because "the best" is an evaluative and subjective notion, it is difficult to distinguish aristocratic from oligarchic or timocratic governments objectively.

Because a monarchical system has its own aristocracy and because the people try to elect the best as their rulers in democracies, an aristocratic element also is present in these regimes. For these reasons, the term "aristocracy" often is used to mean the ruling upper layer of a stratified group. Thus, the upper ranks of the government form the political aristocracy of the state, the stratum of the highest religious dignitaries constitutes the aristocracy of the church, and the richest captains of industry and finance constitute an aristocracy of economic wealth.

The Brahman caste in India, the Spartiates in Sparta, the *eupatridae* in Athens, the patricians or Optimates in Rome, and the medieval nobility in Europe are various historical examples of the social aristocracy or nobility. Most such social aristocracies both legally and factually have been hereditary aristocracies. Other aristocracies have been nonhereditary and recruited from different strata of the population, such as the upper stratum of the Roman Catholic Church, the ruling

Prince Michael of Kent (second from right) *attending the Royal Ascot horse race in 2012. A cousin to Queen Elizabeth II, Prince Michael is a member of the British monarchy's aristocracy.* Max Mumby/Indigo/Getty Images

aristocracy of elective republics and monarchies, the leaders of scientific and artistic organizations, and certain aristocracies of wealth.

The distinction between aristocracy of birth and nonhereditary aristocracy is relative because even in caste societies some low-born persons climb into the higher castes and some high-born persons slide into the lower castes. On the other hand, even in open aristocracies there is a tendency for the upper stratum to become a hereditary group filled mainly by the offspring of aristocratic parents. For example, among millionaires and billionaires living in the United States at the beginning of the 21st century, the percentage born of wealthy parents is notably higher than among American millionaires of the mid-19th century.

Nobles and Gentlemen

Between persistent poverty and the prevailing aristocratic spirit several connections can be made. The strong appeal of noble status and values was a force working generally against the pursuit of wealth and the investment that was to lead, precociously and exceptionally in Britain, to the Industrial Revolution. In France a nobleman could lose rank (*dérogeance*) by working, which inhibited him from engaging in any but a few specified enterprises. The typical relationship between landed gentleman and peasant producer was still feudal; whether represented by a range of rights and dues or by the more rigorous form of serfdom, it encouraged acceptance of the status quo in agriculture. Every state in Europe, except some Swiss cantons, recognized some form of nobility whose privileges were protected by law. Possession of land was a characteristic mark and aspiration of the elites.

The use of the two terms "nobleman" and "gentleman" indicates the difficulty of definition. The terms were loosely used to mark the essential distinction between members of an upper class and the rest. In France, above knights and esquires without distinctive title, ranged barons, viscounts, counts, and marquises, until the summit was reached with dukes and princes of the blood. In Britain, by contrast, only peers of the realm, whether entitled duke, marquess, earl, or baron, had corporate status: numbering under 200, they enjoyed few special privileges beyond membership of the House of Lords. The gentry, however, with assured social position, knighthoods, armorial bearings, and estates, were the equivalent of Continental nobles. With the nobility, they owned more than three-quarters of the land: in contrast, in France by 1789 the nobility owned barely a third. In northern and eastern Europe, where the social structure was generally simpler than in the west, nobles—*dvoriane* in Russia, *szlachta* in Poland and Hungary—were numerous. In these countries, many of those technically noble were in reality of little importance and might even, like the "barefoot *szlachta*," have no land.

Such differences apart, there were rights and privileges that most Continental nobles possessed and values to which most subscribed. The right to wear a sword, to bear a crested coat of arms, to retain a special pew in church, to enjoy such precedence on formal occasions as rank prescribed, and to have, if necessary, a privileged form of trial would all seem to the noble inherent and natural. As landowner he enjoyed rights over peasants, not least as judge in his own court. In France, parts of Germany, Italy, and Spain, even if he did not own the land, he could as lord still benefit from feudal dues. He could hope for special favours from his sovereign or other patron in the form of a pension or office. There were vital exemptions, as from billeting soldiers and—most valuable— from taxation.

The effectiveness of governments can be measured by the extent to which they breached this principle: in France, for example, in the 18th century by the *dixième* and *vingtième* taxes, effectively on income; belatedly, in Poland, where no-bles paid no tax until the chimney tax of 1775. Generally they could expect favourable treatment: special schools, privileges at university, preferment in the church, commissions in the army. They could assume that a sovereign, while encroaching on their rights, would yet share their values. Cardinal Riche-lieu's policy exemplifies such ambivalence. A noble himself, Richelieu, who was chief minister to King Louis XIII of France from 1624 to 1642, sought to promote the interests of his class while directing it toward royal service and clip-ping the wings of the over-powerful. Frederick II the Great of Prussia was not concerned about faction. Since "most commoners think meanly," he believed that nobles were best suited to serve in the government and the army. Such admiration for noble virtues did not usually extend to the political role. The decline of Continental estates and diets, with the growth of bureaucracies, largely recruited from commoners, did not mean, however, even in the west, that nobility was in retreat before the rise of the bourgeoisie. Through social preeminence, nobles maintained—and in the 18th century even tightened—their hold on the commanding heights in church and state.

Within all countries there was a distinction between higher and lower levels within the caste: in some, not only between those who were titled and the rest but, as in Spain and France, between *titulos* and *grandees*, a small group upon which royal blood or the achievement of some ancestor conferred privileges of a self-perpetuating kind. "The grandeeship of the

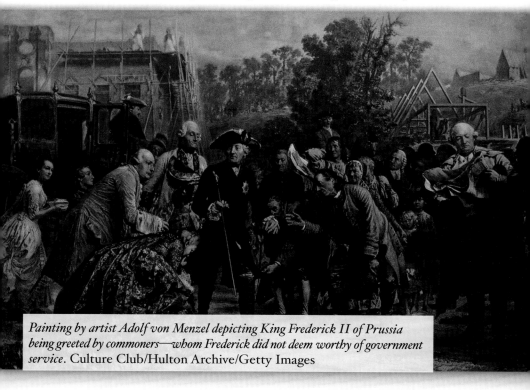

Painting by artist Adolf von Menzel depicting King Frederick II of Prussia being greeted by commoners—whom Frederick did not deem worthy of government service. Culture Club/Hulton Archive/Getty Images

counts of Lemos was made by God and time," observed the head of the family to the new Bourbon king Philip V. No less pretentious were the Condés or the Montmorencys of France. There was a tendency everywhere to the aggrandizement of estates through arranged marriage, a sovereign's favour, or the opportunities provided by war, as in Bohemia after the suppression of the revolt of 1618 or in England with the rise of the Whig families of Russell and Cavendish. In Britain, the principle of primogeniture ensured succession to the eldest son (promoting social mobility as younger sons made their way in professions or trades). Peter I the Great of Russia legislated for the entail (1714), but without success: it was abandoned by Anna (1731) in favour of the traditional law of inheritance. However, *mayorazgo* in Castile and *fideicommissum* in parts of Italy kept vast estates together. Where the colonization of new lands was not restrained by central government, families like the Radziwiłłs and Wiśniowieckis of Poland acquired huge estates. The *szlachta* of Hungary also cherished privileges as descendants of warriors and liberators. There, Prince

Entail

In feudal English law, entail was an interest in land bound up inalienably in the grantee and then forever to his direct descendants. A basic condition of entail was that if the grantee died without direct descendants the land reverted to the grantor. The concept, feudal in origin, supported a landed aristocracy because it served to prevent the disintegration of large estates through divisible inheritance or the lack of heirs. Statutory reforms in England now permit the owner to convey the entailed land by a simple deed and even by will.

There were entailed estates in the American colonies, principally in the middle and southern colonies, but almost all the states emulated Thomas Jefferson's statute of 1776 for Virginia and abolished entails.

Miklós Esterházy, patron of a private orchestra and of Joseph Haydn, excelled all by the end of the 17th century with his annual revenue of 700,000 florins. In Russia, where wealth was measured in serfs, Prince Cherkanski was reckoned in 1690 to have 9,000 peasant households.

Status increasingly signified economic circumstances. In France, where subtle nuances escaped the outsider, one trend is revealing. The old distinction between "sword" and "gown" lost much importance. Age of title came to mean more for antiquarians and purists than for men of fashion who would not scorn a *mésalliance* if it "manured the land." Most daughters of 18th-century tax farmers married the sons of nobles. The class was open to new creations, usually through purchase of an office conferring nobility. When, in a regulation of 1760, the year 1400 was made a test of antiquity, fewer than 1,000 families were eligible. The tendency was toward the formation of a plutocracy. Nobles came to dominate the church and the army, even to penetrate government, from which it had been the policy of the early Bourbons to exclude them. The noble order numbered about 120,000 families by 1789. By then the nobles, particularly those of the country who seldom came to court, had brought their rearguard action to a climax to preserve their privileges—for example, by Ségur's ordinance of 1781, reserving army commissions to nobles of at least four generations. This "feudal reaction" contributed to the problems of government in the years before the Revolution. In Russia, at the height of the conservative reaction that had already secured the abolition (1762) of the service obligation imposed by Peter I, Catherine II the Great was forced to abandon liberal reforms. The Pugachov rising (1773–74), a major Cossack and peasant rebellion in Russia, alerted landowners to the dangers of serfdom, but it was reckoned that three-fifths of all landowners owned fewer than 20 serfs. The census of 1687 showed that there were half a million nobles in

Spain. But *hidalguia* might mean little more than a Spaniard's estimation of himself. Without a substantial *señorio* (estate), the hidalgo was insignificant.

When "living nobly" meant not working and *hidalgos* or *szlachta* attached themselves to a great house for a coat and a loaf, faction became more dangerous and aristocratic interests more resistant to change. It took courage for a sovereign to tackle the entrenched power of nobility in diets, as did the Habsburg queen Maria Theresa (1740–80) in her Austrian and Bohemian lands. Nowhere in Europe did nobles take themselves more seriously, but they were the readier to accept curtailment of their political rights because they enjoyed a healthy economic position. Vienna's cosmopolitan culture and Baroque palaces were evidence of not only the success of the regime in drawing nobles to the capital but also the rise in manorial rents. Nobles played a decorative role in the most ceremonious court in 18th-century Europe. Charles VI (1711–40) had provided 40,000 posts for noble clients. Maria Theresa, concerned about expense, reduced the number of chamberlains to 1,500. It was left to her son Joseph II to attack noble privileges at every point, right up to the abolition of serfdom.

Maria Theresa of Habsburg drastically reduced the powers held by the the estates of various nobles in 18th-century Austria and Bohemia. A. Dagli Orti/De Agostini/ Getty Images

There was a correlation between the advance of government and the curtailment of noble privilege. Inevitably it was an uneven process, depending much on the resolution of a ruler. In Sweden it was to the poor gentlemen, a high proportion of its 10,000 nobles, that Charles XI had appealed in his successful promotion of absolutist reforms in the 1680s. After 1718 the same conservative force militated against royal government. The aristocratic reaction of the age of liberty saw the reassertion of the traditional principle that the nobility were the guardians of the country's liberties. So the Swedish upper class arrived at the position of their British counterparts and obtained that power, not divorced from responsibility, which was envied and extolled by the *philosophes* who regretted its absence from France and sought consolation in the works of Montesquieu. A central idea of his *L'Esprit des lois* (1748; *The Spirit of Laws*) was that noble privilege was the surest guarantee of the laws against despotism. That could not be said of Prussia, although a Junker's privilege was wedded to a subject's duty. In exchange for the loss of political rights, Junkers had been confirmed in their social and fiscal privileges: with the full rigour of serfdom (*Leibeigenschaft*) and rights of jurisdiction over tenants went a secure hold over local government. Under the pressure of war and following his own taste for aristocratic manners, Frederick II taught them to regard the army or civil service as a career. But Frederick disappointed the *philosophes* who expected him to protect the peasantry. The nobles meanwhile acquired a pride in militarism that was to be potent in the creation of the 19th-century German state. The class became more numerous but remained relatively poor: Junkers often had to sell land to supplement meagre pay. Frederick's working nobility sealed the achievements of his capable predecessors. The price paid indicates the difficulties inherent in any attempt to reconcile the interests of the dominant class to the needs of society.

Nobility also had a civilizing role. Europe would be immeasurably poorer without the music, literature, and architecture of the age of aristocracy. The virtues of classical taste were to some extent those of aristocracy: splendour restrained by formal rules and love of beauty uninhibited by utilitarian considerations. There was much that was absurd in the pretensions of some patrons; illusions of grandeur are rarely the best basis for the conceiving of great art. The importance of bourgeois patronage should not be overlooked, otherwise no account would be taken of Holland's golden age. Where taste was unaffected by the need for display (as could not be said of Louis XIV's Versailles) or where a wise patron put his trust in the reputedly best architect, art could triumph. Civilizing trends were prominent, as in England, where there was a free intellectual life. New money, as lavished by the duke of Chandos, builder of the great house of Canons and patron of the composer George Frideric Handel, could be fruitful. Also important was the fusion of aristocratic style with ecclesiastical patronage, as could occur where noblemen enjoyed the best preferment and abbots lived like nobles: the glories of the German Baroque at Melk, Ottobeuren, and Vierzehnheiligen speak as much of aristocracy as of the Christian Gospel.

In contrast with Sweden, where, in the 18th century, talent was recognized and the scientists Carolus Linnaeus and Emanuel Swedenborg were ennobled, or France, where the plutocracy encountered the Enlightenment without discomfort, the most sterile ground for aristocratic culture was to be found where there was an enforced isolation, as in Spain or Europe's poor marches and remotest western shores. Visitors to Spain were startled by the ignorance of the men and the passivity of the women. Life in Poland, Hungary, and Ireland resolved itself for many of the gentry into a simple round of hunting and carousing. The urban aspect of noble culture needs stress, which is not surprising when its Classical inspiration is recalled. Even in England, where educated men favoured country life and did not despise the country town, society would have been poorer without the intense activity of London. All the greater was the importance of the capital cities—Warsaw, St. Petersburg, Budapest, and Dublin—in countries that might not otherwise have generated fine art or architecture.

The aristocratic spirit transcended frontiers. For the nobleman Europe was the homeland. Italian plasterers and painters, German musicians, and French cabinetmakers traveled for high commissions. There were variations reflecting local traditions: the Baroque style was interpreted distinctively in Austria, Italy, Spain, and France. But high style reveals certain underlying principles and convictions. The same is true of the intellectual life of Europe, reflecting as it did two main sources, French and English. It was especially to France that the two most powerful rulers of eastern Europe, Frederick II and Catherine II, looked for mentors in thought and style. The French language, deliberately purified from the time of Richelieu and the foundation of the Academy, was well adapted to the clear expression of ideas. The salons stimulated the discussion of ideas and engendered a distinctive style. Feminine insights there contributed to a rational culture that was also responsive to the claims of sensibility.

Royalty and Gentry

The aristocracy could also be called "the ruling class" because they are the entitled few born into a position of power over others, with regard to both governmental control and high social status. At the top of this ruling class are members of royal families, headed by the king/queen. A succession of titled nobility forms the gentry, which is a collective term for the upper classes.

Monarchs

More commonly referred to as kings and queens, monarchs are the supreme rulers of a nation or territory. They are of higher rank than any other secular ruler except an emperor, to whom a king may be subject. For the purposes of this article, the emphasis will be placed on kings, rather than the female counterpart, queen.

Kingship, a worldwide phenomenon, can be elective, as in medieval Germany, but is usually hereditary; it may be absolute or constitutional and usually takes the form of a monarchy, although dyarchies have been known, as in ancient Sparta, where two kings ruled jointly. The king has often stood as mediator between his people and their god, or, as in ancient Sumer, as the god's representative.

Sometimes he himself has been regarded as divine and has become the key figure in fertility rituals; such religions often ultimately required the death either of the king himself or of an official substitute as a sacrifice to the gods. The concept of divinity, brought in from Egypt, characterized the Hellenistic Age and was later revived by the Roman emperors. The Christian Roman emperors assumed authority as representatives of God, and, in medieval political theory, kingship was early regarded as to some extent analogous with the priesthood, the ceremony of anointing at the coronation becoming highly significant. The absolute monarchies of the 16th to 18th century were often strengthened by the establishment of nationalist churches; but from the 17th century in England and, later, in other countries, kingship was made constitutional, royal power being held to derive from the people rather than from God.

Prince and Princess

Prince and princess are European titles of rank, usually denoting a person exercising complete or almost complete sovereignty or a member of a royal family, but in some cases used to designate high-ranking nobles. The role of princes in various European nations, as well as Russia and Poland, in medieval times was to assist the king by governing parts of the regent's land, known as principalities.

France

Although lordly vassals might conventionally be referred to as "princes," the title of prince was not official in France until the 15th century, when members of the royal house came to be distinguished as "princes of the blood" (*princes du sang*) with specified rights of precedence; in 1711 they were granted precedence absolutely.

In a few cases the king accorded or acknowledged the title without defining the status of a principality in relation to a duchy, a countship, or a marquisate. Such princely titles were often borne by the eldest sons of dukes.

Germany

From the 10th to the 12th century a new class of *Fürsten*, or princes, arose in Germany, consisting of the holders of well-defined territorial lordships in immediate dependence on the German king and on the Holy Roman Empire. An Estate of Princes of the Realm (*Reichsfürstenstand*) came into being from the 1180s and comprised dukes, counts palatine, margraves, landgraves, archbishops, bishops, certain abbots, and the masters of the military-religious orders. New admissions to this estate required not only the sovereigns' bestowal of the title *Fürst* (lower than that of duke or landgrave) but also the consent of the existing princes. In the *Reichstag*, or Diet, the *Kurfürsten*, or electoral princes (more commonly, electors), eventually set themselves apart from the others, whose number grew considerably until the dissolution of the Holy Roman Empire. Only 10 princes were not mediatized by 1815—including Liechtenstein, which even survived World Wars I and II. The title of *Fürst* as bestowed by the Prussian monarchy in the 19th–20th century was simply honorific.

The German language uses the term *Fürst* for a prince with sovereign or quasi-sovereign rights or for the head of a princely family, but it may use *Prinz* for a junior member of a sovereign or princely house. Examples are *Kronprinz*, crown prince; *Kurprinz*, electoral prince, heir to an electorate; *Erbprinz*, hereditary prince, heir to a principality; Prinz von Preussen, heir presumptive to Prussia; and Prinz von Battenberg, for descendants of the grand ducal house of Hesse through a morganatic marriage.

Spain and Portugal

In Spain, counts of Barcelona had been regarded as princes of Catalonia in the sense that they were the greatest feudatories of that country. When Count Ramón Berenguer IV became king-consort of Aragon in 1137, he styled himself Príncipe de Aragon instead of king. The sons of Spanish kings, meanwhile, had the style of *infante*; but the title of Príncipe de Asturias was created, in 1388, for the eldest son of John I of Castile, the future Henry III of Castile. On the union of the Castilian and Aragonese crowns, this title became that of the heir apparent to the whole Spanish monarchy; it long remained the only Spanish princely title. In 1795, however, the title Príncipe de la Paz was created for Manuel de

Baldomero Espartero, the Spanish general who was granted the title Prince of Vergara because of his support of Queen Isabella. The title was created just for him. Time & Life Pictures/Getty Images

Godoy, with higher rank than his duchy of La Alcudia; but it was abolished in 1808. Baldomero Espartero received the title Príncipe de Vergara in 1872 for his lifetime only. Outside Spain, on the other hand, the Spanish kings bestowed princely titles with extreme liberality.

In Portugal the heir apparent to the throne had the title of Prince Royal from the reign of King Edward (1433–38).

Italy

In southern Italy the Lombard dukes of Benevento became practically sovereign princes after the Frankish annexation of the northern kingdom of Lombardy (774); successive partitions of their territory, from 847, created three principalities—Benevento, Salerno, and Capua. In the 11th century the latter two fell to the Normans, while Benevento became an exclave of the Papal States. Subsequently, princely titles became very numerous in southern Italy: the Spanish kings conceded at least 120 for Sicily and about as many for Naples. For Italy as a whole the aggregate was increased by Roman principalities created by the papacy and by principalities of the Holy Roman Empire in the north.

Great Britain

In Great Britain the word "prince" could always be used in a generally descriptive way for a monarch, duke, or other major peer with intrinsic judicial powers; but as a title of rank it was not used until 1301, when Edward I invested his son, the future Edward II, as Prince of Wales. (From Edward III's time the king's eldest son and heir was usually so invested.) Essentially, a prince originally was one who was sovereign in his or her territories, and the word is transgender—Mary, Queen of Scots, in her correspondence described herself as "a freeborn prince."

Not until the accession of the German George I (1714), however, did it become settled practice for all the sovereign's descendants in the male line (that is, his children and the children of his sons) to be styled prince or princess and royal highness; great-grandchildren in the male line were prince or princess and highness. Before that, in both England and Scotland, the children of the monarchs were styled as Lord Forename or Lady Forename. In 1917 George V limited the title of prince or princess to the sovereign's children and the children of the sovereign's sons; the only extension was for the eldest living son of the eldest son of the Prince of Wales. The granting or withholding of a princely style and title remained, however, a matter of the sovereign's will: Queen Elizabeth II's consort, Philip, Duke of Edinburgh, was expressly created a prince of Great Britain and Northern Ireland in 1957.

Russia and Poland

In Russia and in Poland the title prince was accorded to descendants of sovereign or formerly sovereign dynasties, whether Russian, Tatar, Lithuanian, or Polish. Apart from this use, the title was granted as a high rank of nobility by the Russians from Peter the Great's time (1682–1725).

In Poland 10 princely houses claimed descent from ancient dynasties; four more were created by the Holy Roman Empire and one was created by the Holy See, in addition to one created in 1808 by the Russians, but only two were created for ordinary nobles by the Polish crown (Poniatowski in 1764, Poninski in 1773).

Duke and Duchess

Duke (the feminine being duchess) is a European title of nobility, having ordinarily the highest rank below a prince or king (except in countries having such titles as archduke or grand duke).

The title of *dux*, given by the Romans to high military commanders with territorial responsibilities, was assumed by the barbarian invaders of the Roman Empire and was used in their kingdoms and also in France and Germany for rulers of very large areas. The early Carolingian sovereigns in France and in Germany continued to appoint dukes, but their weaker successors found themselves increasingly constrained to free the dukes from royal control in the areas that they had to defend.

Germany

Franconia, Swabia, Bavaria, and Saxony, originally the homes of distinct tribes, emerged as the great "stemduchies" of Germany when the dukes appointed by the Carolingians as military governors made themselves increasingly independent.

In the 12th century the Hohenstaufen emperors, who created the new duchies of Austria (1156) and Styria (1180), seemed likely to succeed in reducing the dukes to genuinely obedient vassalage. At the same time, the lesser noble families began to consolidate their own holdings and jurisdiction at the expense of the ducal authority. The growth of these smaller territorial principalities (countships, etc.) naturally diminished the real prestige of the dukes. Despite the collapse of the Hohenstaufen design after 1250 and the success of the dukes in securing their independence in their own principalities, their title came no longer to denote greater power under the king but to signify only a higher rank than that of the princely counts. Furthermore, with the extensive privileges accorded the electors (only one of whom was a duke) by the Golden Bull of 1356—the constitution of the Holy Roman Empire that was designed, in part, to recognize the importance of the empire's princes, particularly the electors—the duke had ceased even in theory to be the highest-ranking of the princes of the empire; the Austrian dukes indeed assumed the new title of archduke, claiming equal rights with electors.

From the 16th to the 19th century, lords of even comparatively small territories were granted or took the ducal title. Eleven duchies survived until 1918: Oldenburg, the two Mecklenburgs (east and west), Saxe-Weimar (as the grand duchy of Saxony), Baden, and Hesse-Darmstadt were grand duchies; and Anhalt, Brunswick, Saxe-Altenburg, Saxe-Meiningen, and Saxe-Coburg-Gotha were sovereign duchies.

France

The dukes of Normandy, Aquitaine, and Burgundy were practically independent of the French crown in the early feudal period, as also was the duke of Brittany, though the French royal chancellery at first accorded him only the style of count. Gradually, however, these great fiefs were reunited to the French crown. Thereafter they were granted only in *appanage*, as *duchés-pairies*, or peerage duchies—initially to princes of the blood royal but, from the 16th century onward, also to bastard princes of the blood, to foreign princes, and to other noble subjects of the French king. *Duchés-pairies* were hereditary, but there were also hereditary duchies that were not peerage titles, as well as life duchies (*à brevet*, or *par lettres*). Apart from those in the royal house of France, there were more than 30 ducal titles dating from the *ancien régime* still being borne (unofficially) in the 1980s, the premier duchy of France being that of Uzès (1565; registered 1572).

Italy

The great territorial duchies of Italy that survived into modern times were those of Milan, Florence (as the grand duchy of Tuscany), Lucca, Mantua, Modena, and Parma-Piacenza. The popes, the emperors, and the kings of Naples, however, could all bestow the ducal title as they wished and often did so; consequently, the title is now fairly widespread. The kings of the house of Savoy gave the title of *duca* occasionally to their offspring.

Spain

The Visigothic duchies of Spain disappeared after the Muslim conquest. During the Christian reconquest the title of *duque* was revived for honorific purposes. Apart from the Castilian duchy of Soria y Molina, created in 1370 for Bertrand du Guesclin, the title was at first usually reserved for royal princes, but, from the middle of the 15th century onward, it was accorded more and more frequently to other nobles. Of these latter creations, the premier surviving is that of Medina Sidonia (1445). The Spanish kings also created duchies very liberally in their Neapolitan and Sicilian dominions. By virtue of the right accorded to him by the Cortes, General Francisco Franco created three duchies in 1948: those of Calvo Sotelo, of Mola, and of Primo de Rivera.

Portugal

John I of Portugal created the duchies of Coimbra and Viseu for his sons Dom Pedro and Dom Henrique after their capture of Ceuta from the Moors in 1415, and in 1442 he created the duchy of Bragança for his illegitimate son Afonso. Six more duchies were created for branches of the royal house before the Spanish annexation of Portugal. Thereafter duchies were accorded outside the royal house, but the total number of creations was far smaller than in Spain.

The British Isles

There were no English ducal titles (the duchies of Normandy and Aquitaine held by the English kings being, of course, French fiefs) until 1337, when Edward III erected the county of Cornwall into a duchy for his son Edward, the Black Prince. There followed the duchies of Lancaster (1351), Clarence (1362), York (1385), Gloucester (1385), Bedford (1st creation; 1413), and Somerset (1st creation; 1443), all for descendants of the royal house in the male line. In 1444, however, Humphrey Stafford, of royal blood only through his mother, was made Duke of Buckingham (1st creation). After the creation of the dukedom of Norfolk in 1483, the title became increasingly recognized as not being reserved for the royal blood.

In Scotland the title was first bestowed in 1398 by Robert III on his eldest son, David, who was made Duke of Rothesay, and on his brother Robert, Duke of Albany.

The effigy from the tomb of Edward, Prince of Wales, also known as the Black Prince. The duchy of Cornwall was created for him by his father, King Edward III. Hulton Archive/Getty Images

Lords and Ladies

In the British Isles, lord was a general title for a prince or sovereign or for a feudal superior (especially a feudal tenant who holds directly from the king, i.e., a baron). In the United Kingdom the title today denotes a peer of the realm, whether or not he sits in Parliament as a member of the House of Lords. Before the Hanoverian succession, before the use of "prince" became settled practice, royal sons were styled Lord Forename or the Lord Forename.

The prefix "lord" is ordinarily used as a less formal alternative to the full title (whether held by right or by courtesy) of marquess, earl, or viscount and is always so used in the case of a peerage baron (particularly in the peerage of Scotland, where it remains the only correct usage at all times). Where the name is territorial, the "of" is dropped—thus the Marquess of A. but Lord A. The younger sons of a duke or marquess have, by courtesy, the title of lord prefixed to their forename and surname—e.g., Lord John Russell (as a younger son of the Duke of Bedford). The form of address "my lord" is not used for lords of the manor, a position that accords no rank or title.

The feminine of lord is lady, which is a general title for any peeress below the rank of duchess and also for the wife of a baronet or of a knight. Before the Hanoverian succession, when the use of "princess" became settled practice, royal daughters were styled Lady Forename or the Lady Forename. "Lady" is ordinarily used as a less formal alternative to the full title of a countess, viscountess, or baroness; where the name is territorial, the "of" is dropped—thus the Vicountess of A. but Lady A. The daughters of dukes, marquesses, and earls also have, by courtesy, the title of lady prefixed to their forename and surname—e.g., Lady Jane Grey.

In the late 20th century, apart from royal dukedoms, there were nine dukedoms in the peerage of England, eight in the peerage of Scotland, six in the peerage of Great Britain, two in the peerage of Ireland, and six in the peerage of the United Kingdom. However, some dukes presided over multiple duchies. As a result, the total 31 ducal titles provided only 26 dukes.

Marquess

Also spelled marquis (in France and from time to time in Scotland), marquess is a European title of nobility, ranking in modern times immediately below a duke and above a count, or earl. Etymologically the word "marquess" or "margrave" denoted a count or earl holding a march, or mark, that is, a frontier district; but this original significance has long been lost. The feminine form of marquess is marchionessa.

In western Europe the Carolingian marchiones or margraves had been royal officials whose duty of defending a frontier might justify an exception being made to the normal rule that no count should hold more than one countship, or county. Their authority was thus not much less than that of a duke; indeed the term *Markherzog* ("mark duke") is occasionally found instead of *Markgraf* ("mark count"). But as conditions on the frontiers or the frontiers themselves were changed, the special importance of the old marches diminished.

France

As the great French feudatories' power grew at the expense of the king's, the old *marquisats* were practically lost in the great duchies or countships. Then, with the multiplication of little fiefs, minor counts holding several such lordships took to assuming the style of marquis to distinguish themselves. The rank of a marquis, always inferior to that of a duke, was thus in a controversial relation to that of a count.

Sometimes a count's nobility was better established and his fief greater than that of any marquis; sometimes a marquis with a royal patent should obviously have precedence. These ambiguities served to bring the title into disrepute in the 17th and 18th centuries, as being too often self-made or pretentious (the frequency of its unauthorized adoption creating the French verb *se marquiser*). After the Revolution had abolished the rank, Napoleon did not see fit to revive it. Louis XVIII, reviving it after the Restoration, gave its holders definitive precedence between dukes and counts.

Germany

At the end of the Carolingian era, the German kings of the Saxon dynasty, Otto I, Otto II, and Otto III, created a new system of marks in the 10th century, giving particular attention to their eastern frontier. A margrave was expected not only to secure the frontier but also to push it forward into Slav or pagan territory, as did Gero, the Billungs, the margraves of Meissen, and Albert I (the Bear). Some of the margravates developed into hereditary principalities; thus, the Bavarian Ostmark became the duchy of Austria, the Steiermark became the duchy of Styria, and the Saxon Nordmark became the electorate of Brandenburg. Later, however, the margraves of Baden were so styled simply because their ancestors had held the mark of Verona in 11th-century Italy; the Hohenzollern margraves of Ansbach and of Bayreuth likewise echoed their ancestors' title to Brandenburg.

Italy

The frontier mark in Italy long survived as a major territorial unit, though the original Carolingian demarcations were substantially altered. By the 14th century, however, barons and *signori* had begun to erect their fiefs into *marchesati*, after which the title grew to have much the same fate as the French *marquisat*.

Spain

The remnant of the original Carolingian Marca Hispanica was merged in the countship of Barcelona. The first Castilian *marquesado* was that of Villena (on the Valencian frontier), created for Don Alonso of Aragon in 1376; the Pacheco family, who acquired it from the crown in 1445, subsequently became dukes of Escalona. The next senior *marquesado* was that of Santillana (1445).

The British Isles

In England the Late Latin term *marchiones* was early applied to the lords of the Welsh marches, but it was there used in a sense descriptive only of their lordships' location near the frontier without implying that they were superior to other earls. In 1385, however, Robert de Vere, 9th Earl of Oxford, was created Marquess of Dublin with precedence between dukes and earls; the other earls resented this creation, and the patent of the marquessate was revoked in 1386, after its holder had been created Duke of Ireland. John Beaufort, Earl of Somerset, was created Marquess of Dorset and of Somerset in 1397, but he was degraded to his former earldom in 1399. When the Commons petitioned for his restoration as Marquess of Dorset in 1402, he objected because of the strangeness of the term in England. In 1443, however, his son Edmund Beaufort was raised to be Marquess of Dorset, after which the title retained its place in the peerage. As earlier creations became extinct or were raised to dukedoms, the premier marquessate of England in the 20th century was that of Winchester, created in 1551.

Count

Counts are members of European nobility, as are their feminine counterparts known as countesses. The title is equivalent to a British earl, ranking in modern times after a marquess or, in countries without marquesses, a duke. The Roman *comes* was originally a household companion of the emperor, while under the Franks he was a local commander and judge. The counts were later slowly incorporated into the feudal structure, some becoming subordinate to dukes, although a few counties (or countships), such as those of Flanders, Toulouse, and Barcelona, were as great as duchies. The reassertion of royal authority over the feudatories, which took place at different times in the different kingdoms and led to the formation of centralized states of the modern type, meant that most counts lost their political authority, though they retained their privileges as members of the nobility.

France

French counts became vassals of dukes by 900 at the latest; but, as the process of feudalization continued, the counts tended to lose their official character and to become the hereditary lords of little territories. In France this development is already discernible in the 11th century, and with its devaluation there arose the practice of applying the title of count very loosely. By the 12th century any lord of moderate status might style himself count, no less than the truly great feudatories of Flanders and Toulouse; and even in the 13th century, when the organization of the French kingdom became more stable, the title might mean much or comparatively little.

The development of the system of royal *bailliages* from the beginning of the 13th century onward served progressively to restrict the counts' rights of legislation, judiciary, and private war. (Later, in the 16th century, the counts lost their right to mint money.) Moreover, gradually the great fiefs were reunited under the French crown, after which they were granted only in appanage (the territory itself being administered as a province of the kingdom); counts simply retained various privileges. Later countships, under the First Empire and the subsequent monarchies and empire, had no territorial significance but were made hereditary in order of primogeniture.

Germany

Although in Germany the title of count (*Graf*) had become hereditary in most cases as early as the 10th century, the counts retained something of an official character rather longer than in France. In the 12th century, however, seemingly by Emperor Frederick I (Barbarossa), they were given authority to maintain the public peace in the district under their control—an authority that until 1100 had belonged to the dukes. Thenceforward the term "countship" signified the territory within which the count had powers of life and death.

From the beginning of the 12th century, a number of counts appeared in western Germany, taking their titles simply from the castles they held and having no obvious connection with any official status. In Frederick Barbarossa's time certain freemen of the higher class, such as *Vögte*, or "advocates," began to style themselves as counts. In the 13th and

14th centuries there are instances of new countships received as fiefs from dukes.

Within the Holy Roman Empire there gradually developed distinctions between ordinary counts and counts of the empire (*Reichsgrafen*), who became members of the college of counts (*Grafenkollegium*), a component of the Diet of the empire. After the dissolution of the Holy Roman Empire in 1806, the counts of the empire were mediatized—i.e., made subject to the sovereigns of the various German states instead of being "immediate" subjects of the emperor alone. The federal Diet, in 1829, however, recognized their right to the special style of Erlaucht ("Illustrious Highness").

Italy

With the decay of Carolingian authority, a system of countships based on cities grew up in Italy. Probably none were dependent on dukes, the ducal title being then comparatively rare, especially in northern Italy. The rise of communes meant the end of the countship's former significance, but as a mark of privilege, the title of count was quite liberally bestowed by the popes and other sovereigns of the peninsula well into modern times.

Spain

In Spain the countship developed under Visigothic influence in the kingdom of Asturias-León and under Frankish influence in Catalonia and in the country immediately south of the Pyrenees. By uniting the Catalan countships, the counts of Barcelona made themselves into near sovereign princes, comparable at least to the powerful counts of Flanders and Toulouse; and the Carolingian countship of Aragon was the nucleus of the kingdom of that name. The countship of

Castile, on the other hand, from which the kingdom of Castile emerged, was originally a frontier district of the kingdom of Asturias-León. Here the official character of the counts as district administrators appointed by the kings was preserved until the end of the 11th century, when the principle of hereditary lordships of one sort or another emerged and ultimately prevailed. Under the Spanish monarchies of the Renaissance and later, the title of count was infrequently conferred.

Russia and Poland

In Russia, where the title of count was not introduced until Peter the Great's time, it came to be given usually to officials of a certain rank in the government service. In Poland there were no counts before the partitions of the late 18th century, when the title was introduced by the Russians, Austrians, and Prussians.

England's Earls

The title of earl (the English equivalent of count, from the Danish *jarl*) was first introduced into England under King Canute of Denmark and of Norway (king of England 1016–35), but prior to this the duties of an earl, the administration of a shire or province on behalf of the king, were performed by ealdormen. Earl is thus the oldest title and rank of English nobles extant today. It was also the highest until as late as 1337, when Edward, the Black Prince, was created Duke of Cornwall by his father, Edward III.

Initially the earls wielded administrative authority over several (modern) counties, but, after the Norman Conquest in 1066, the earl's duties were theoretically restricted to a single county, although some were earls of more than one county. Under the Norman kings earldoms became hereditary, but their representation of the king was lost to the sheriffs, and then in 1328, with the creation of Roger Mortimer as Earl of March, the essential association of earldoms with specific territories was abandoned. From the 18th century the practice developed of simply adding the grantee's surname (imitating a style of the 11th–12th centuries, when, for example, the Earl of Buckingham was styled Earl Giffard), so that the style of the Earl of Place-name was now supplemented by that of Earl Surname.

The rules of succession to earldoms were originally those for the inheritance of fiefs in feudal law, so that, for example, an earldom might pass to a woman, her husband receiving the title of earl in her right, but from the reign of Richard II earldoms could be created for life (Sir Guichard d'Angle, Earl of Huntingdon in 1377) or with inheritance limited to male heirs. By the 1963 Peerage Act, an earl, in common with other British peers, may, within one year of inheriting his title, renounce it for life; then, during his lifetime, it remains dormant.

Scotland's Earls

While England's shires were ruled for the king by ealdormen, the Pictish provinces in the north of what subsequently became Scotland were ruled by the mormaers, the Great Stewards. At the beginning of the 12th century, in the reign of Alexander I, they became known as earls, seven of whom formed a Carolingian style of peerage known as the Seven Earls of Scotland. With the adoption of the Saxon title of earl (undoubtedly owed to the influence of Alexander's Saxon mother, the sainted Queen Margaret) and its integration with the Celtic mormaer, these powerful men added a personal title of dignity to their territorial title and judicial status. Their successors under Alexander's brother, King David I, were integrated into the Flemish-Norman system of feudalism so that the lands for which they were responsible, and which had been held by the tribes they ruled, now became their own as tenants-in-chief of the crown. More earldoms were created in the following reigns, until there were 13, but the Seven Earls (chosen as needed from the eventual 13) had become a constitutional and privileged body of great power acting as guardians of the realm and principal lay advisers to the king. However, at the end of the 13th century, at the time England's King Edward I was attempting to subdue and conquer Scotland, the political turmoil was such that the power of the earls was reduced to that of those of England.

Viscount

Ranking immediately below a count (or earl) is the viscount, the feminine of which is viscountess. In the Carolingian period of European history, the *vicecomites*, or *missi comitis*, were deputies, vicars, or lieutenants of the counts, whose official powers they exercised by delegation. As the countships eventually became hereditary, the lieutenancies did as well: for instance, in France the viscounts in Narbonne, in Nîmes, and in Albi appear to have made their office hereditary by the beginning of the 10th century. Even so, viscounts remained for some time with no other status than that of the count's officers, either styling themselves simply *vicecomites* or qualifying their title with the name of the countship whence they derived their powers.

France

By the end of the 11th century, the universal tendency of feudalism to associate status with the possession of land caused the French viscounts to qualify their title with the name of their own most important fief. In Aquitaine, of which the counts of Poitiers were dukes, and in the county of Toulouse the viscounts were great barons often able to assert themselves against their suzerain. In the Île-de-France, in Champagne, and in part of Burgundy, on the other hand, the viscounts by the end of the 12th century were surviving only as minor feudatories, having lost their special administrative functions to the *prévôts*.

In Normandy, however, the judicial functions of the viscounts as deputies of the duke remained important for some time longer. By the middle of the 11th century most of the country was administratively divided into *vicecomtés* (this explains the Norman use of the Latin term *vicecomes* for the sheriff in England); under Henry I of England the hereditary holders of the *vicomtés* in his Norman possessions were to a large extent replaced by ducal officials.

British Isles

In England the viscountcy was not introduced into the peerage until four centuries after the Norman Conquest: John, Lord Beaumont, who had been created Count of Boulogne in 1436, was in 1440 created Viscount Beaumont in the peerage of England, with precedence over all barons. The oldest English viscountcy surviving today is that of Hereford, created in 1550; the premier Irish one, however, that of Gormanston, is somewhat older, having been created in 1478. The premier viscount in the peerage of Scotland is the Viscount of Falkland, whose peerage title was created in 1620.

Spain

Viscounts had been created in Catalonia by Charlemagne in the 8th century, whence the title had spread, with diminishing functions and increasingly significant noble rank, to Aragon and to Castile. Philip IV of Spain introduced the system of *vizcondados previos* (regulations of 1631 and of 1664); under this, no one could proceed to the rank of *conde* (count) or *marqués* (marquess) unless he had previously been *vizconde*. A fee of 750 ducats had to be paid for this habilitating title (except in the case of counts' sons), and a further fee of 750 ducats was required for the obligatory cancellation of the *vizcondado* when the time came to confer the higher rank. The removal of the obligation to cancel, in 1846, led only to confusion, as numerous families began petitioning to have their already cancelled titles revived; in 1858 it was declared that the *vizcondado previo* was no longer necessary for accession to the higher titles.

Baron

Baron, or the feminine baroness, is a title of nobility, ranking below a viscount (or below a count in countries without viscounts). In the feudal system of Europe, a baron was a "man" who pledged his loyalty and service to his superior in return for land that he could pass to his heirs. The superior, sovereign in his principality, held his lands "of no one"—i.e., independently—and the baron was his tenant-in-chief. In early feudal times the baron in turn, in a process of subinfeudation, might have had his own subordinate barons. This practice was discontinued in England when King Edward I recognized the political and fiscal dangers it posed.

Great Britain

In England the Norman kings assembled advisory councils of the more powerful barons. As these councils evolved into Parliaments larger numbers of barons, as well as representatives of the church, burgesses, and knights of the shires, were summoned to attend the meetings.

The early baron held his lands, or barony, of the king; if the lands passed from his family they carried away the rank and the privileges of that rank: such barons were termed barons by tenure. After the concept of the peerage—those titled individuals who shared the responsibility of government—began to develop, those feudal barons by tenure who had received writs summoning them to the early Parliaments were considered to be ipso facto peers, barons by writ. Landless men who were created peers in anticipation of their contributions to the crown were termed barons by patent. Letters patent (grants made publicly) became the usual way to create new peers or to promote existing ones.

Initially the distinction between barons by tenure and those who were the equivalent of peers was unclear. The rank was conferred along with the holdings in the feudal system, but through the hierarchy of feudal ranks the barons held baronies, the lords held lordships, and the earls held earldoms in the same relationship of fealty to the sovereign, *in baroniam*.

The subsequent slow decline of the law-enforcing powers of the barons so reduced the importance of the baronies that the term "baron" became at one time in Scotland a synonym for freeholder, while in England the term became a title for those in the lowest rank of the peerage. Life peers, whose rank is not heritable, are styled baron. In Scotland today a baron is still one who holds a feudal rank, and the lowest rank of the Scots peerage, equivalent to the rank of baron in the peerages of England, of Great Britain, of Ireland, and of the United Kingdom, is lord of parliament.

France

In 12th-century France the term "baron," in a restricted sense, was applied properly to all lords possessing an important fief, but toward the end of the 13th century the title had come to mean that its bearer held his principal fief direct from the crown and was therefore more important than a count, since many counts were only mediate vassals. From this period, however, the title tended to sink in importance. In the 14th century the barons were ranked below counts and viscounts, though in power and possessions many barons were superior to many counts. In any case, until the 17th century the title of baron could be borne only by the holder of a territorial barony, and it was Louis XIV who first cheapened the title in France by creating numerous barons by royal letters. The creation of barons was later revived by Napoleon I, continued by Louis XVIII, Charles X, and Louis-Philippe, and revived again on a generous scale by Napoleon III. Since 1870 the tolerant attitude of the French republican governments toward titles, which are not officially recognized, has increased the confusion by facilitating the assumption of the title on very slender grounds of right.

Germany

The German equivalent of baron, *Freiherr*, or "free lord" of the empire, originally implied a dynastic status, and many *Freiherren* held countships without taking the title of count (*Graf*). When the more important of them styled themselves counts, the *Freiherren* sank into an inferior class of nobility. The practice of conferring the title of *Freiherr* by imperial letters— begun in the 16th century by Emperor Charles V—was later exercised by all the German sovereigns.

Italy

In the Middle Ages the Italian barons had extensive powers of jurisdiction within their domains and could inflict the death penalty. There was a right of appeal, but it was of little value generally and in Sicily and Sardinia was nonexistent. In the late Middle Ages the barons' powers became more extensive, especially in the south, and they had the right to mint money and wage private war. The title was recognized until 1945.

Spain

In early medieval Navarre and Aragon *barón* described the senior nobility but later, perhaps under the influence of Castilian practice, it was displaced by *ricos hombres*— "rich men." In Catalonia a baron was simply a magnate, but in the later Middle Ages he achieved a distinct status even more important than the French barons. Some nobles retained the title until it was abolished by the Cortes of Cadiz in 1812.

CHAPTER 4

THE RISE AND DECLINE OF FEUDALISM IN WESTERN EUROPE

Historians have pointed to a loss of centralized power in the domains overseen by Carolignian rulers, as well as the need to protect their kingdoms, as the overarching reason for the advent of feudalism in Europe. Likewise, there are general factors attributed to fedualism's decline. During the 12th century a cultural and economic revival took place. The balance of economic power slowly began to shift from the region of the eastern Mediterranean to western Europe. Towns began to flourish, and merchant classes began to develop. The population therefore rapidly expanded, a factor that eventually led to the breakup of the old feudal structures.

More specifics behind how the feudal system took hold—and what contributed to its demise—in various European countries are covered in this chapter.

The Roots of German Feudalism

Because the Carolingians—a term that refers to the family of Frankish aristocrats descended from Pippin and Charlemagne and the dynasty they established to rule western Europe—were unable to provide effective defense for the whole kingdom, military command and the political and economic power necessary to support it necessarily devolved to local leaders whose regions were attacked. The inevitable result was the decentralization and decay of royal authority to the benefit of the regional dukes. Contrary to popular opinion, these dukes were not appointed by their peoples, nor were they descendants of the tribal chieftains of the postmigration period. The so-called *Stammesherzogtümer* (tribal duchies) were new political and, ultimately, social units. Their dukes were Carolingian counts, part of the international "imperial aristocracy" of the Carolingians, who organized defense on a local basis without questioning loyalty to the Carolingians.

All the same, their initial success established them in the hearts of those whom they protected. In Saxony the Liudolfings, descendants of military commanders first established by Louis the German, achieved spectacular successes against the Slavs, Danes, and Magyars. In Franconia the Konradings rose to prominence over this largely Frankish region with the assistance of Arnulf but became largely independent during the minority of his son. Similarly, the Luitpoldings, originally named as Carolingian commanders, became dukes of Bavaria. Thuringia fell increasingly under the protection and lordship of the Liudolfings. In Swabia (Alemannia) several clans disputed control with one another and with regional ecclesiastical lords. Throughout the kingdom the only force for preserving unity remained the church, but the bishops approved the secularization of much monastic land to sustain troops who could counter the threat of external foes, thus further strengthening the power of the dukes.

The structural transformation of the "imperial aristocracy" into a local elite accompanied the emergence of an increasingly particularist, dynastically oriented aristocratic society that was bound together through ties of vassalage and in which local rulers exercised personal lordship over the free and half-free populations of the regions. This process did not advance as far in Germany as it did in France. Everywhere German society remained closer to older, regional varieties of social organization as well as to traditions of Carolingian government by ecclesiastical authorities and imperial deputies.

Lords and Peasantry in Medieval Germany

Despite the impressive advance of trade and industry in the later Middle Ages, German society was still sustained chiefly by agriculture. Of an estimated population of 12 million in 1500, only 1.5 million resided in cities and towns.

Agriculture exhibited strong regional differences in organization. The more recently settled areas of the north and east were characterized by great farms and extensive estates that produced a surplus of grain for export through the Baltic ports. The south and west was a region of denser population, thickly sown with small villages and the "dwarf" estates of the lesser nobility. In the northeast the great landlords, headed by the Knights of the Teutonic Order, tightened their control over the originally free tenants, denied them freedom of movement, and ultimately bound them to the soil as serfs. In the south the heavy urban demand for grain chiefly benefited the

Archduke Eugen of Austria, in robes as the last grand master of the Teutonic Order. Teutonic Knights were large landholders in the Middle Ages. A. Dagli Orti/De Agostini/Getty Images

larger peasant proprietors, who sold their surplus production in the nearest town and used their gains to acquire more land. The lesser peasantry, with their smaller holdings, practiced chiefly subsistence farming, produced no surplus, and therefore failed to benefit from the buoyant urban demand.

Transformation of Rural Life

The frequent division of the patrimony among heirs often reduced it to uneconomically small fragments and encouraged an exodus to the cities. On the other hand, landless day labourers who survived the Black Death in the mid-14th century were able to command higher wages for their services.

In southern Germany the strain of transition in rural society was heightened by the policies of the landlords, both lay and ecclesiastical. Confronted by labour shortages and rising costs, many landlords attempted to recoup their losses at the expense of their tenants. By means of ordinances passed in the manorial courts, they denied to the peasantry their traditional right of access to commons, woods, and streams. Further, they revived their demands for the performance of obsolete labour services and enforced the collection of the extraordinary taxes on behalf of the prince.

The peasants protested and appealed to custom, but their sole legal recourse was to the manorial court, where their objections were silenced or ignored. Ecclesiastical landlords were especially efficient, and peasant discontent assumed a strong anticlerical tinge and gave rise to the localized disturbances in Gotha (1391), Bregenz (1407), Rottweil (1420), and Worms (1421). Disturbances recurred with increasing frequency in the course of the 15th century on the upper Rhine, in Alsace, and in the Black Forest. In 1458 a cattle tax imposed by the archbishop of Salzburg kindled a peasant insurrection, which spread to Styria, Carinthia, and Carniola.

The Demise of Serfdom in Eastern Europe

Conditions for eastern European peasants in the 14th century do not seem to have been worse than those of the west, and in some ways they were better, because the colonization of forestlands in eastern Germany, Poland, Bohemia, Moravia, and Hungary had led to the establishment of many free-peasant communities. But a combination of political and economic circumstances reversed these developments. The chief reason was that the wars that devastated eastern Europe in the 14th and 15th centuries tended to increase the power of the nobility at the expense of the central governments. In eastern Germany, Prussia, Poland, and Russia, this development coincided with an increased demand for grain from western Europe. To profit from this demand, nobles and other landlords took back peasant holdings, expanded their own cultivation, and made heavy demands for peasant labour services.

Peasant status from eastern Germany to Muscovy consequently deteriorated sharply. Not until the late 18th century were the peasants of the Austro-Hungarian Empire freed from serfdom, thus recovering their freedom of movement and marriage and the right to learn a profession according to personal choice. The serfs of Russia were not given their personal freedom and their own allotments of land until Alexander II's Edict of Emancipation of 1861.

In Alsace the malcontents formulated a series of specific demands, which included the abolition of the hated manorial courts and the reduction of feudal dues and public taxes to a trifling annual amount. On these fundamental points there was little room for compromise, and the outbreaks were stifled by the heavy hand of established authority. But the rigours of repression added fuel to peasant discontent, which finally burst forth in the great uprising of 1524–25.

The Revolution of 1525

The events of the revolutionary years 1524–25 were labeled a "peasant rebellion," but modern scholarship has made it clear that the insurrection was far more than a series of uprisings by rural bands. The tens of thousands of peasants drawn into the movement, some of them massed in major military actions, were a symptom of the general unrest that had gripped Germany since the middle of the 15th century. Both peasants and city dwellers resented the concentration of land and economic and political power in the hands of the landed nobility and wealthy merchants, as well as the burden of the tributes, taxes, and forced labour that these elites exacted. The growth of the population heightened these resentments by causing a shortage of available land, particularly in the south, and driving up prices and rents. The particular demands pressed in the 1520s—mitigation of fiscal and labour burdens imposed on peasants by their lords, autonomy for village communes, and relief from high taxes—had been voiced before.

In the regions involved—Franconia, Swabia, the Upper Rhine and Alsace, Thuringia, and Tirol—large forces of peasants attacked castles, monasteries, and some cities. News of these actions encouraged discontented urban groups to rise against their oligarchic town governments, and for a while it looked as though a united revolutionary front of ordinary—i.e., nonprivileged—people might be forged. Manifestos and lists of articles abounded; there was talk everywhere of judging things by "God's law" (meaning the Gospel), and some groups even laid plans for a "Christian association" across regional and urban-rural lines. But before long the forces of the propertied won the upper hand, and the insurrectionaries were put down with the ferocity customary in those days.

Moving Toward Lasting Reform

The emperor Joseph II (1765–90), a well-meaning though doctrinaire reformer, attempted to initiate a revolution from above against the opposition of powerful forces that continued to cling to tradition. In the course of a single decade he tried to centralize the government of his far-flung domains, reduce the influence of the church, introduce religious toleration, and ease the burden of serfdom. His uncompromising program of innovation, however, alienated the landed aristocracy, whose support was essential for the effective operation of the government. The emperor encountered mounting unrest, which did not end until his death in 1790, and the subsequent abandonment of most of the reforms that he had promulgated.

It wasn't until the dawn of the 19th century that Germany officially abolished the remains of its feudal system. Between 1806 and 1813 the statesmen in Berlin initiated a revolution from above to transform a rigid despotism into a popular monarchy supported by the loyalty of a free citizenry. Among the most important achievements of German reformers at this time was the abolition of serfdom, a measure designed to create citizens out of human beasts of burden. Yet, while the reforms gave the peasant personal freedom, they failed to provide him with economic independence. Most of the land remained in the hands of the aristocracy, which therefore continued to dominate the countryside politically as well as socially.

The Genesis of Feudalism in France

A foremost circumstance of the later 9th and the 10th century was the inability of the western Frankish Carolingian kings to keep order. The royal estates that had theretofore supported them, mostly in the north and east, were depleted through grants to retainers uncompensated by new acquisitions. Hindered by poor communications, the kings lost touch with lesser counts and bishops, while the greater counts and dukes strove to forge regional clienteles in fidelity to themselves. These princes (as they were called) were not rebels. More often allied with the king than not, they exercised regalian powers of justice, command, and constraint; it was typically they who undertook to defend local settlements and churches from the ravages of Magyars invading from the east, of Muslims on Mediterranean coasts, and of Vikings from northern waters.

Of these invaders, the Northmen, as contemporaries called the Vikings, were the most destructive. They raided landed estates and monasteries, seizing provisions and movable wealth. Striking as far inland as Paris by 845, they attacked Bordeaux, Toulouse, Orléans, and Angers between 863 and 875. From a base in the Somme estuary, they pillaged Amiens, Cambrai, Reims, and Soissons. But they were drawn especially to the Seine valley. Between 856 and 860 they laid waste to the country around its lower reaches and repeatedly attacked Paris thereafter. Sometimes they were turned back by defenses but more often by payments of tribute. After 896 the invaders began to settle permanently in the lower Seine valley, whence they spread west to form the duchy of Normandy. Maritime raiding continued into the 10th century, then subsided.

Lords such as the counts of Flanders, Paris, Angers, and Provence were well situated to prosper in the crisis. They were often descended from or related to Carolingian kings. Adding protectorates over churches to their inherited offices, domains, and fiefs while acquiring other lordships and counties through marriage, they built up principalities that were as precarious as they were powerful. The lords tried to avoid dismemberment of the patrimony by limiting their children's right of succession and marriage, but it was only in the 12th century that these dynastic principles came to prevail in the French aristocracy. The princes, moreover, found it almost as hard as the kings to secure their power administratively. They exploited their lands through servants valued less for competence than for fidelity; these servants, however, were men who tended to think of themselves as lords rather than agents. This tendency was especially marked among the masters of castles (castellans), who by the year 1000 were claiming the power to command and punish as well as the right to retain the revenues generated from the exercise of such power. In this way was completed a devolution of power from the undivided empire of the 9th century to a checkerboard of lordships in the 11th—lordships in which the control of castles was the chief determinant of success.

The devolution of power led to a fragmented polity; at every level lords depended on the services of sworn retainers who were usually rewarded with the tenures of lordship called fiefs (*feuda*). In the 9th century fiefs were not yet numerous enough to undermine the public order protected by kings and their delegates. Indeed, fiefs were at first rewards for public service made from fiscal (royal) lands; this practice persisted in the south into the 11th century. By then, however, castles, knights, and knights' fiefs were multiplying beyond all control, resulting in a fracturing of power that few princes succeeded in reversing before 1100. Counts were unwilling to admit that their counties were fiefs or that they owed the same sort of allegiance to kings or dukes as their vassals did to them. Tainted with servility as well as with the brutality of needy knights on the make, vassalage was slow to gain

Feudalism in Medieval Spain

Feudal ideas emphasizing private and personal relationships exerted great influence on the governmental and military organization of the Christian kingdoms of medieval Spain—most fully in Catalonia, where French influence was strong. As vassals holding fiefs of the count of Barcelona, the Catalan nobles owed him military and court service, and they often had vassals of their own.

Illustration showing a skirmish during the Rebellion of the Remences, a peasant uprising in medieval Catalonia.
Universal Images Group/Getty Images

In the western states, royal vassals usually held land in full ownership rather than in fief. As vassals of the king or count, the magnates, called *ricos hombres* (i.e., rich or powerful men) in the west and *barones* in Catalonia, functioned as his chief counselors and provided the bulk of the royal military forces. Nobles of the second rank, known variously as *infanzones*, *caballeros*, or *cavallers*, generally were vassals of the magnates.

Agriculture and pasturage were the principal sources

of wealth in the Christian states, as the king, landlords, and nobles gained their income primarily through the exploitation of landed property. Peasants dwelling on noble estates cultivated the soil and owed various rents and services to their lords. The serfs (*solariegos* in Castile, *payeses de remensa* in Catalonia), who were effectively bound to the land, bore the heaviest burden. The rights (the so-called "evil usages") of Catalan lords were such that they could abuse their serfs at will.

Castilian peasants living on lands known as *behetrías* were free to choose their lord and to change their allegiance whenever they wished, but their right to do so was challenged in the 13th century. Life on the frontier attracted many peasants because, while it exposed them to risk and adventure, it also promised freedom. Like pioneers in all ages, they developed a strong sense of personal worth and independence.

respectability. The multiplication of fiefs was a violent process of subjugating free peasants and abusing churches.

Effect of the French Revolution

The revolutionary movement that shook France between 1787 and 1799 marked the end of the *ancien régime* in France. Although historians disagree on the causes of the Revolution, several reasons are commonly adduced. One reason is that the increasingly prosperous elite of wealthy commoners—merchants, manufacturers, and professionals, often called the bourgeoisie—produced by the 18th century's economic growth resented its exclusion from political power and positions of honour. Also, the peasants were acutely aware of their situation and were less and less willing to support the anachronistic and burdensome feudal system.

An undated coloured engraving depicting an armed mob of Parisians storming the Bastille on July 14, 1789, at the start of the French Revolution. Photos.com/Thinkstock

By any standard, the fall of the Bastille to the Parisian crowd on July 11, 1789, was a spectacular symbolic event—a seemingly miraculous triumph of the people against the power of royal arms. The heroism of the crowd and the blood of its martyrs—ordinary Parisian artisans, tradesmen, and workers—sanctified the patriot cause. Most important, the elites and the people of Paris had made common cause, despite the inherent distrust and social distance between them.

Peasant Insurgencies

Peasants in the countryside, meanwhile, carried on their own kind of rebellion, which combined traditional aspirations and anxieties with support of the patriot cause. The peasant revolt was autonomous, yet it reinforced the urban uprising to the benefit of the National Assembly.

Competition over the ownership and use of land had intensified in many regions. Peasants owned only about 40 percent of the land, leasing or sharecropping the rest from the nobility, the urban middle class, and the church. Population growth and subdivision of the land from generation to generation was reducing the margin of subsistence for many families. Innovations in estate management—the grouping of leaseholds, conversion of arable land to pasture, enclosure of open fields, division of common land at the lord's initiative, discovery of new seigneurial (of the feudal lord) dues or arrears in old ones—exasperated peasant tenants and smallholders.

Historians debate whether these were capitalistic innovations or traditional varieties of seigneurial extraction, but in either case the countryside was boiling with discontent over these trends as well as over oppressive royal taxes and food shortages. Peasants were poised between great hopes for the future raised by the calling of the Estates-General and extreme anxiety—fear of losing land, fear of hunger (especially after the catastrophic harvest of 1788), and fear of a vengeful aristocracy.

In July peasants in several regions sacked the castles of nobles and burned the documents that recorded their feudal obligations. This peasant insurgency eventually merged into the movement known as the Great Fear. Rumours abounded that these vagrants were actually brigands in the pay of nobles, who were marching on villages to destroy the new harvest and coerce the peasants into submission. The fear was baseless, but hundreds of false alarms and panics stirred up hatred and suspicion of nobles, led peasants to arm themselves as best they could, and set off widespread attacks on châteaus and feudal documents. The peasant revolt suggested that the unity of the Third Estate against "aristocrats" extended from Paris to villages across the country. The Third Estate truly seemed invincible.

The Abolition of Feudalism in France

Of course the violence of peasant insurgency worried the deputies of the National Assembly; to some it seemed as if the countryside were being engulfed by anarchy that threatened all property. But the majority were unwilling to turn against the rebellious peasants. Instead of denouncing the violence, they tried to appease peasant opinion. Liberal nobles and clergy began the session of August 4 by renouncing their ancient feudal privileges. Within hours the Assembly was propelled into decreeing "the abolition of feudalism" as well as the church tithe, venality of office, regional privilege, and fiscal privilege. A few days later, to be sure, the Assembly clarified the August 4 decree to assure that "legitimate" seigneurial property rights were maintained. While personal feudal servitudes such as hunting rights, seigneurial justice, and labour services were suppressed outright, most seigneurial dues were to be abolished only if the peasants paid compensation to their lords, set at 20 to 25 times the annual value of the obligation. The vast majority of peasants rejected that requirement by passive resistance, until pressure built in 1792–93 for the complete abolition of all seigneurial dues without compensation.

The abolition of feudalism was crucial to the evolution of a modern, contractual notion of property and to the development of an unimpeded market in land. But it did not directly affect the ownership of land or the level of ordinary rents and leases. Seigneurs lost certain kinds of traditional income, but they remained landowners and landlords. While all peasants gained in dignity and status, only the landowning peasants came out substantially ahead economically. Tenant farmers found that what they had once paid for the tithe was added on to their rent. And the Assembly did virtually nothing to assure better lease terms for renters and sharecroppers, let alone their acquisition of the land they tilled.

The Introduction of Feudalism in England

The Norman Conquest of England, which began in 1068, has long been a matter of debate. The question has been whether the Norman ruler, William I, introduced fundamental changes in England or based his rule solidly on Anglo-Saxon foundations. A particularly controversial issue has been the introduction of feudalism. On balance, the debate has favoured dramatic change while also granting that in some respects the Normans learned much from the English past. Yet William replaced his initial policy of trying to govern through

Etching of William I, who some historians believe introduced the concepts of feudalism to England. Print Collector/Hulton Archive/Getty Images

Englishmen with an increasingly thoroughgoing Normanization.

The Conquest resulted in the subordination of England to a Norman aristocracy. William probably distributed estates to his followers on a piecemeal basis as lands came into his hands. He granted lands directly to fewer than 180 men, making them his tenants in chief. Their estates were often well distributed, consisting of manors scattered through a number of shires. In vulnerable regions, however, compact blocks of land were formed, clustered around castles.

The tenants in chief owed homage and fealty to the king and held their land in return for military service. They were under obligation to supply a certain number of knights for the royal feudal host—a number that was not necessarily related to the quantity or quality of land held. Early in the reign many tenants in chief provided knights from their own households to meet demands for service, but they soon began to grant some of their own lands to knights who would serve them just as they in turn served the king. They could not, however, use their knights for private warfare, which, in contrast to Normandy, was forbidden in England.

In addition to drawing on the forces provided by feudal means, William made extensive use of mercenary troops to secure the military strength he needed. Castles, which were virtually unknown in pre-Conquest England and could only be built with royal permission, provided bases for administration and military organization. They were an essential element in the Norman settlement of England.

The upper ranks of the clergy were Normanized and feudalized, following the pattern of lay society. Bishops received their lands and the symbols of their spiritual office from the king. They owed knight service and were under firm royal control.

"Bastard" feudalism

The so-called Wars of the Roses were the struggle between the Yorkist and Lancastrian descendants of Edward III for control of the throne and of local government. The origins of the conflict have been the subject of much debate. It can be seen as brought about as a result of Henry VI's inadequacy and the opposition of his dynastic rival Richard, Duke of York, but local feuds between magnates added a further dimension. Because of the crown's failure to control these disputes, they acquired national significance. Attempts have been made to link these civil conflicts to what is known as "bastard" feudalism, the system that allowed magnates to retain men in their service by granting them fees and livery and made possible the recruiting of private armies. Yet this system can be seen as promoting stability in periods of strong rule as well as undermining weak rule such as that of Henry VI.

Commerce, Disease, and Discontent

By the 14th century, economic conditions in western Europe were favourable to the replacement of serfs by a free peasantry. The growth of the power of central and regional governments permitted the enforcement of peasant-landlord contracts without the need for peasant servility, and the final abandonment of labour services on demesnes removed the need for the direct exercise of labour discipline on the peasantry. The drastic population decline in Europe after 1350 as

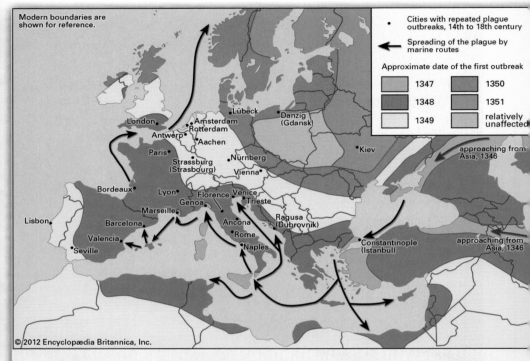

The reach of the Black Death in Europe from 1347 to 1351 can be seen as it spreads year by year. Encyclopædia Britannica, Inc.

a result of the Black Death left much arable land uncultivated and also created an acute labour shortage, both economically favourable events for the peasantry.

Finally, the endemic peasant uprisings in western Europe during the 14th and 15th centuries also forced more favourable terms of peasant tenure. Although the new peasants were not necessarily better off economically than were their servile forebears, they had increased personal liberties and were no longer entirely subject to the will of the lords whose lands they worked.

The Black Death

The Black Death was the pandemic that ravaged Europe between 1347 and 1351, taking a proportionately greater toll of life than any other known epidemic or war up to that time. Some scientific evidence has indicated that the Black Death may have been viral in origin. However, the disease is more widely believed to have been the result of plague, caused by infection with the bacterium *Yersinia pestis*. Consequently, the origin of modern plague epidemics lies in the medieval period.

Originating in China and Inner Asia, the plague was transmitted to Europeans in or around 1347 when a Kipchak army, besieging a Genoese trading post in the Crimea, catapulted plague-infested corpses into the town. The disease spread from the Mediterranean ports, affecting Sicily and mainland Italy, Spain, England, France, North Africa, Austria, Hungary, Switzerland, Germany and the Low Countries, and Scandinavia and the Baltic lands.

The rate of mortality from the Black Death varied from place to place. The population in England in 1400 was perhaps half what it had been 100 years earlier; in that country alone, the Black Death certainly caused the depopulation or total disappearance of about 1,000 villages. A rough estimate is that 25 million people in Europe died from plague during the Black Death. The population of western Europe did not again reach its pre-1348 level until the beginning of the 16th century.

One lasting and serious consequence of the Black Death was the drastic reduction of the amount of land under cultivation, due to the deaths of so many labourers. This proved to be the ruin of many landowners. The shortage of labour compelled them to substitute wages or money rents in place of labour services in an effort to keep their tenants. There was also a general rise in wages for artisans and peasants. These changes brought a new fluidity to the hitherto rigid stratification of society.

Feudalism in Medieval Italy

Early medieval Italy was an overwhelmingly agrarian society, as it had been before and as it was to be for centuries. Wealth thus derived above all from the ownership of landed estates. Estates were exploited by subsistence tenants on a standard medieval pattern. The slave plantations of 1st-century central Italy had long disappeared, and the word *servus* now usually just meant a tenant without public rights as a freeman; the remaining slaves on the land were mostly skilled specialists. Free and servile tenants essentially paid rent, in money or kind, to their landlords.

For the late 8th and 9th centuries, at least in northern Italy and Tuscany, there is evidence of more organized estates, which were the equivalent of the manors of England and the *villae* of 9th-century northern France. Here tenants also had to work without pay on the lord's demesne, an area whose produce went entirely to the lord. These estates, mostly royal or ecclesiastical, could be huge. They produced a sizable agricultural surplus, which the estates' owners often sold in the cities (Santa Giulia, at least, had its own merchants). Not all estates, however, were organized this tightly; elsewhere demesnes, though common, tended to be smaller and less economically important; and in the south they were always rare.

The existence of this stratum of free smallholders gave a certain reality to the Lombard, and indeed Frankish, constitutional tradition that based royal power on the nation of free warriors at arms. The rise of the aristocracy, however, gravely challenged this tradition. Already in the Lombard period the aristocracy was in practice politically dominant, and probably always had been, in patterns unbroken from the Gothic and Roman period. Yet the 8th-century aristocracy does not seem to have been as wealthy as either its Roman predecessors or its Carolingian and post-Carolingian successors, and this may imply a relative independence for the free peasantry. Under Charlemagne and his descendants, this slowly changed. Incoming Frankish nobles acquired large lands, and churches dramatically increased their holdings. That these developments were often at the expense of the poor is shown by a number of 9th-century court cases in which peasants claimed their land, or sometimes their freedom, usually without success; in some of these cases, peasants were clearly in the right. Kings themselves confirmed this, for in the 9th century they worried greatly that the oppressions of the poor would lessen the latter's participation in the public obligations of all freemen—army service, attendance at court, and road and bridge building—and they made laws against such exploitations. The laws were futile, however, and aristocratic landowning and political dominance continued to grow.

In the 10th century, with the breakdown in royal power, these tendencies developed further. In the countryside, castles became the centres of de facto political power that great landowners exercised over their free neighbours. A new, highly militarized small nobility began to emerge, based on these castles. Their ancestors had been of mixed origins—vassals of counts, local diocesan landowners, and even rising free peasants—but they now held, as a group, a virtual monopoly over armed force; indeed, in the sources they are frequently called *milites* ("soldiers"). Counts, where they kept their own power, did so only as leaders of private armies of these *milites*, who, though still their vassals, were now much more autonomous. Churches, to keep control over their extensive lands, had to give much of it out in lease or fief to such military families, and only the strongest churchmen, such as the archbishop of Milan, managed to keep any real power over their new military dependents.

This new castle-holding stratum was to become the basic aristocratic class of the 11th to 13th centuries, with only a few of them aspiring to the official titles of count or viscount. Such a tendency was, in fact, common throughout Europe; in Italy the chief difference was that *milites* were never quite as dominant as elsewhere, for cities remained powerful political and military centres, and peasant owners continued to exist in the countryside. The major exception to this was probably the south, where the new pattern of fortified settlements kept the peasantry within a more rigid political framework than existed in the more scattered villages of the north. Even within such a framework of political control, however, some of these fortified villages achieved a new sort of prosperity, for artisans could work in them, and merchants would come there, too.

Italian Landholder Reform

Changes in the character of the economy in town and country profoundly affected the development of both the republics and the *signorie*, or Italian lords. Although scholars today often contend that in this period an "urban economy" drove northern and central Italy, in contrast to the rest of Europe, most Italians still lived on the land, and the prosperity of any town depended greatly on its *contado*, or the rural territory that it governed. Here, despite differences in agriculture due to different climates and types of soil, certain patterns of development occurred within the peninsula.

By the end of the 13th century, tenurial serfdom had virtually died away, and other forms of landholding were evolving to take its place. Sometimes peasants worked the land as freeholders (as in fact many peasants had always done, even at the very height of the manorial system). Sometimes (and this was particularly true of large ecclesiastical estates in northern Italy) lands were let out on perpetual hereditary lease for low rents—a procedure that, in effect, often led to the virtual dispossession of church proprietors in favour of secular tenants. But the most common new tenancy from the 13th century was that in which landlords offered short-term leases in return for heavy rents either in money or, more often, in kind. Among such leases the one that came to figure most prominently, especially in well-cultivated land in central and northern Italy, was sharecropping, particularly *mezzadria*. In contracts of *mezzadria*, the landlord provided half the seed sown and in return received half of the tenant's fruits. Frequently the contract was renewable every year—a provision that held considerable insecurity for the lessee, who was obligated to leave the land at term. Often, in order to make sure that the landlord received a full return from his lease, detailed conditions were attached on rotation of crops, plowing, digging, and harrowing. In all, this form of tenure, which was to remain a central feature of northern Italian rural life up to the mid-20th century, can be seen less as an agreement to let land than one to hire labour.

CHAPTER 5

FEUDAL SOCIETIES OF ASIA

The concept of feudalism—in terms of a social and political hierarchy that dictated land ownership and use—existed long before it was common in medieval Europe. Systems of land tenure in exchange for service and protection were instituted in several ancient Asian societies, including China and Japan. On the Asian subcontinent, the Hindu caste system as practiced in India has many elements of a feudatory society.

The Chinese Feudal State

The vast time sweep of the Zhou dynasty—encompassing some eight centuries—is the single longest period of Chinese history. The Zhou dynasty ruled ancient China for almost a millennium, establishing the distinctive political and cultural characteristics that were to be identified with China for the next 2,000 years.

The beginning date of the Zhou has long been debated. Traditionally, it has been given as 1122 BCE, and that date has been successively revised as scholars have uncovered more archaeological evidence. The most recent findings have placed the outright start of the dynasty at 1046 BCE. During the Xi (Western) Zhou (1046–771 BCE), the first of the two major divisions of the period, the Zhou court maintained a tenuous control over the country through a network of feudal states. This system broke down during the Dong (Eastern) Zhou (770–256 BCE), however, as those states and new ones that arose vied for power.

The Zhou coexisted with the Shang for many years, living just west of the Shang territory in what is now Shaanxi province. At various times they were a friendly tributary state to the Shang, alternatively warring with them. One of the Zhou ruling houses devised a plan to conquer the Shang, and a decisive battle was fought, probably in the mid-11th century. Before the whole Shang territory could be consolidated by the Zhou, a rebellion broke out. The fighting went on for three years before the rebellion was put down, and finally the Zhou solidified their reign over all of China. An array of feudal states was created within the empire to maintain order and the emperor's hold on the land.

The Zhou Feudal System

During the rule of the Zhou, an eastern capital was constructed on the middle reach of the Huang He (Yellow River) as a stronghold to support the feudal lords in the east. Several states established by Zhou kinsmen and relatives were transferred farther east and northeast as the vanguard of expansion, including one established by the son of Zhougong. The total number of such feudal states mentioned in historical records and later accounts varies from 20 to 70; the figures in later records would naturally be higher, since enfeoffment (to invest with a fief) might take place more than once. Each of these states included fortified cities. They were strung out along the valley of the Huang He between the old capital and the new eastern capital, reaching as far as the valleys of the Huai and Han rivers in the south and extending eastward to the Shandong Peninsula and the coastal area north of it. All these colonies mutually supported each other and were buttressed by the strength of the eastern capital, where the conquered Shang troops were kept, together with several divisions of the Zhou legions. Ancient bronze inscriptions make frequent mention of mobilizing the military units at the eastern capital at times when the Zhou feudal states needed assistance.

Each of the Zhou feudal states included fortified cities. They were strung out along the valley of the Huang He between the old capital and the new eastern capital, reaching as far as the valleys of the Huai and Han rivers in the south and extending eastward to the Shandong Peninsula and the coastal area north of it. All these colonies mutually supported each other and were buttressed by the strength of the eastern capital, where the conquered Shang troops were kept, together with several divisions of the Zhou legions. Ancient bronze inscriptions make frequent mention of mobilizing the military units at the eastern capital at times when the Zhou feudal states needed assistance.

The feudal states were not contiguous but rather were scattered at strategic locations surrounded by potentially dangerous and hostile lands. The fortified city of the feudal lord was often the only area that he controlled directly; the state and the city were therefore identical, both being *guo*, a combination of city wall and weapons. Satellite cities were established at convenient distances from the main city in order to expand the territory under control. Each feudal state consisted of an alliance of the Zhou, the Shang, and the local population. A Chinese nation was formed on the foundation of Zhou feudalism.

The scattered feudal states gradually acquired something like territorial solidity as the neighbouring populations established closer ties with them, either by marriage or by accepting vassal status; the gaps between the fortified cities were thus filled by political control and cultural assimilation. This created a dilemma for the Zhou central court: the evolution of the feudal network buttressed the structure of the Zhou order, but the strong local ties and parochial interests of the feudal lords tended to pull them away from the centre. Each of these opposing forces became at one time or another strong enough to affect the history of the Zhou order.

For about two centuries Zhou China enjoyed stability and peace. There were wars against the non-Zhou peoples of the interior and against the nomads along the northern frontier, but there was little dispute among the Chinese states themselves. The southern expansion was successful, and the northern expansion worked to keep the nomads away from the Chinese areas.

Examples from the Zhou Court

The changing strength of the feudal order can be seen from two occurrences at the Zhou court. In 841 BCE the nobles jointly expelled Liwang, a tyrant, and replaced him with a collective leadership headed by the two most influential nobles until the crown prince was enthroned. In 771 BCE the Zhou royal line was again broken when Youwang was killed by invading barbarians. The nobles apparently were split at that time because the break gave rise to two courts, headed by two princes, each of whom had the support of part of the nobility. One of the pretenders, Pingwang, survived the other, but the royal order had lost prestige and influence. The cohesion of the feudal system had weakened.

The Chunqiu Period

The familial relationship among the nobles gradually was diluted during the Chunqiu period. A characteristic of the Zhou feudal system was that the extended family and the political structure were identical. The line of lordship was regarded as the line of elder brothers, who therefore enjoyed not only political superiority but also seniority in the family line. The head of the family not only was the political chief but also had the unique privilege of offering sacrifice to and worshipping the ancestors, who would bestow their blessings and guarantee the continuity of the mandate of heaven. After the weakening of the position of the Zhou king in the feudal structure, he was not able to maintain the position of being the head of a large family in any more than a normal sense.

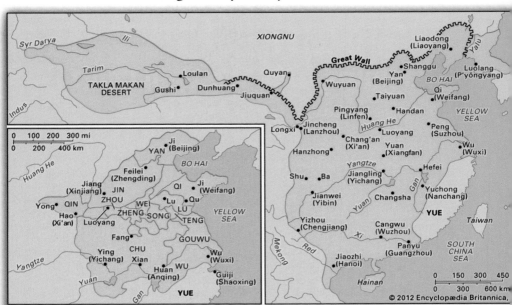

China under the Han emperor Wudi (c. 100 BCE) and (inset) at the end of the Chunqiu (Spring and Autumn) period (c. 500 BCE). Encyclopædia Britannica, Inc.

The feudal structure and familial ties fell apart, continuing in several of the Chunqiu states for various lengths of time, with various degrees of modification. Over the next two centuries the feudal-familial system gradually declined and disappeared.

In the first half of the Chunqiu period, the feudal system was a stratified society, divided into ranks as follows: the ruler of a state; the feudal lords who served at the ruler's court as ministers; the *shi* (roughly translated as "gentlemen") who served at the households of the feudal lords as stewards, sheriffs, or simply warriors; and, finally, the commoners and slaves. The state ruler and the ministers were clearly a superior class, and the commoners and slaves were an inferior class; the class of *shi* was an intermediate one in which the younger sons of the ministers, the sons of *shi*, and selected commoners all mingled to serve as functionaries and officials. The state rulers were, in theory, divided into five grades; in reality, the importance of a ruler was determined by the strength of his state. The ministerial feudal lords, however, often had two or three grades among themselves, as determined by the lord-vassal relationship. In general, each state was ruled by a group of hereditary feudal lords who might or might not be of the same surname as the state ruler.

Leadership Changes

The system was not stable in the Chunqiu period, and everywhere there were changes. The first important change occurred with the advent of interstate leadership. For several decades after 722 BC, the records chiefly show battles and diplomatic maneuvers among the states on the central plain and in the middle and lower reaches of the Huang He valley. These states, however, were too small to hold the leadership and too constricted in the already crowded plain to have potentiality for further development. The leadership was soon taken over by states on the peripheral areas.

The first to achieve this leadership was Huangong (reigned 685–643 BCE), the ruler of the state of Qi on the Shandong Peninsula. He successfully rallied around him many other Chinese states to resist the pressure of non-Chinese powers in the north and south. While formally respecting the suzerainty of the Zhou monarchy, Huangong adopted a new title of "overlord" (*ba*). He convened interstate meetings, settled disputes among states, and led campaigns to protect his followers from the intimidation of non-Chinese powers.

After his death the state of Qi failed to maintain its leading status. The leadership, after a number of years, passed to Wengong of Jin (reigned 636–628 BCE), the ruler of the mountainous state north of the Huang He. Under Wengong and his capable successors, the overlordship was institutionalized until it took the place of the Zhou monarchy. Interstate meetings were held at first during emergencies caused by challenges from the rising southern state of Chu. States answering the call of the overlord were expected to contribute and maintain a certain number of war chariots. Gradually the meetings became regular, and the voluntary contribution was transformed into a compulsory tribute to the court of the overlord. The new system of states under the leadership of an overlord developed not only in northern China under Jin but also in the south under Chu. Two other states, Qin and Qi, though not commanding the strength of the formidable Jin and Chu, each absorbed weaker neighbours into a system of satellite states. A balance of power thus emerged among the four states of Qi, Qin, Jin, and Chu. The balance was occasionally tipped when two of them went to war, but it was subsequently restored by the transference of some small states from one camp to another.

A further change began in the 5th century BCE, when the states of Wu and Yue far to the south suddenly challenged Chu for hegemony over the southern part of China, at a time when the strong state of Jin was much weakened by an internecine struggle among powerful magnates. Wu got so far as to claim overlordship over northern China in an interstate meeting held in 482 BCE after defeating Chu. But Wu's hegemony was short-lived; it collapsed after being attacked by Yue. Yue held the nominal overlordship for only a brief period; Jin, Qin, and Qi were weakened by internal disturbances (Jin split into three contending powers) and declined; and a series of defeats paralyzed Chu. Thus, the balance-of-power system was rendered unworkable.

A half century of disorder followed. Small states fell prey to big ones, while in the big states usurpers replaced the old rulers. When the chaos ended, there were seven major powers and half a dozen minor ones. Among the seven major powers, Zhao, Han, and Wei had formerly been parts of Jin; the Qi ruling house had changed hands; and Qin was undergoing succession problems. The only "old" state was Chu. Even Chu, a southern state, had become almost completely assimilated to the northern culture (except in art, literature, and folklore). The minor powers had also changed: some had retained only small portions of their old territories, some had new ruling houses, and some were new states that had emerged from non-Chinese tribes. The long interval of power struggle that followed (475–221 BCE) is known as the Zhanguo (Warring States) period.

The Decline of Feudalism

The years from the 8th century BCE to 221 BCE witnessed the painful birth of a unified China. It was a period of bloody wars and also of far-reaching changes in politics, society, and intellectual outlook.

The most obvious change in political institutions was that the old feudal structure was replaced by systems of incipient bureaucracy under monarchy. The decline of feudalism took its course in the Chunqiu period, and the rise of the new order may be seen in the Zhanguo period. The Zhou feudalism suffered from a continual dilution of authority. As a state expanded, its nobility acquired vassals, and these in turn acquired their own vassals. The longer this went on, the more diluted the family tie became and the more dependent the ruler became on the combined strength of the vassals. At a certain point, the vassals might acquire an advantageous position, and the most dominant figures among them might eclipse the king.

The Zhou royal house perhaps reached the turning point earlier than the other feudal states. As a result, the Zhou royal domain and its influence shrank when Pingwang moved his court to the east. The ruling houses of other states suffered the same fate. Within a century after the Zhou court had moved to the east, the ruling houses in most of the feudal states had changed. In some cases a dominating branch replaced the major lineage, and in others a powerful minister formed a strong vassaldom and usurped the authority of the legitimate ruler. Bloody court intrigues and power struggles eliminated many established houses. The new power centres were reluctant to see the process continue and therefore refused to allow further segmentation and subinfeudation. Thus, the feudal system withered and finally collapsed.

Japanese Feudalism, in Brief

The Japanese feudal system began to take shape under the Kamakura *bakufu* (hereditary military dictatorship, also known as a shogunate), though it remained only inchoate during the Kamakura period. Warrior-landlords lived in farming villages and supervised peasant labour or themselves carried on agriculture, while the central civil aristocracy and the temples and shrines held huge public lands (*kokugaryō*) and private estates in various provinces and wielded power comparable to that of the *bakufu*. These *shōen* were managed by influential resident landlords who had become warriors. They were often the original developers of their districts who became officials of the provincial government and agents of the *shōen*. Under the Kamakura *bakufu*, many such individuals became *gokenin* and were appointed *jitō* in lands where the *bakufu* were allowed access. As leaders of a large number of villagers, these *jitō* laboured to develop the rice fields and irrigation works in the areas under their jurisdiction, and they and other influential landlords constructed spacious homes for themselves in the villages and hamlets where they lived.

Among these landlords, some were vassals of the shogun, while others were connected to the aristocracy or the temples and shrines. The *jitō* owed their loyalty to the shogun, for whom they performed public services such as guard duty in Kyōto and Kamakura. In return, the shogun not only guaranteed these men security of tenure in their traditional landholdings but rewarded them with new holdings in confiscated lands—such as from the Taira or the supporters of Go-Toba. This connection between lord and vassal, on which grants of landownership or management were based, gave Japanese society a somewhat feudal character.

But these lands were by no means complete fiefs: the Kamakura *bakufu* did not possess large tracts of its own land that it could grant to its vassals as fiefs in return for service. Kamakura warriors could control traditional land types—*shōen* and *kokugaryō*—or be newly appointed into confiscated lands. In either case, there was a nominal absentee central proprietor—temple, shrine, or aristocratic or royal family—who maintained substantial control over the land. Thus, there was a limit on the degree to which the Kamakura warrior could exploit the land and people under his control. Conflict was endemic between central proprietor (usually a local representative of the proprietor) and *jitō*: the former wished to maintain as much control and income as possible while the latter was concerned with expanding his share. Since the *jitō* was entirely under the control of Kamakura, disputes flooded the warrior headquarters from landowners seeking to curtail *jitō* encroachments. Thus, the primary focus of Kamakura activity became the dispensing of justice in legal cases involving land disputes. The Kamakura *bakufu* gained a reputation for fairness, issuing countless orders of admonition to its vassals to follow the precedents on the land in question. By various means, however, Kamakura warriors managed to whittle away significantly the absentee control of *shōen* proprietors.

Conflict also was endemic between the farming population and the warriors, stemming from the efforts of the former to increase personal and economic autonomy, as well as to enlarge their holdings within the *shōen* or *kokugaryō*. There were several different statuses among the peasantry, including *myōshu*, prominent farmers with taxable, named fields (*myōden*) of significant size and long standing; small cultivators with precarious and shifting tenures; and others who paid only labour services to the proprietor or *jitō*. These groups, while distinct from one another, were also quite separate from transient agriculturalists present in many estates. The lowest peasant category, called *genin* ("low person"), was made up of people who were essentially household servants with no land rights.

As members of the Japanese warrior caste, the samurai, in theory, performed military service on the battlefield and during times of peace, in addition to managing agricultural holdings, engaging in hunting and training in the martial arts, and nourishing a rugged and practical character. Medieval texts speak of *kyūba no michi* ("the way of the bow and horse"), or *yumiya toru mi no narai* ("the practices of those who use the bow and arrow"), indicating that there was an emerging sense of ideal warrior behaviour that grew out of this daily training and the experience of actual warfare. Pride of family name was especially valued, and loyal service to one's overlord became the fundamental ethic. This was the origin of the more highly developed sense of a warrior code of later ages. Like his Heian predecessor, the Kamakura warrior was a mounted knight whose primary martial skill was equestrian archery. The status of women in warrior families was comparatively high; like their Heian predecessors, they were allowed to inherit

Samurai on horseback, drawing, late 19th century. Library of Congress, Washington, D.C.

a portion of the estates and even *jitō* posts, a practice that gradually came to be restricted.

After the middle of the Kamakura period, the farming villages in which the warriors resided underwent changes

Samurai

The term "samurai" was originally used to denote the aristocratic warriors, but it came to apply to all the members of the warrior class that rose to power in the 12th century. The ideal samurai was supposed to be a stoic warrior who followed an unwritten code of conduct, which held bravery, honour, and personal loyalty above life itself. Ritual suicide by disembowelment (*seppuku*) was institutionalized as a respected alternative to dishonour or defeat.

In the early part of the Tokugawa period (1603–1867), the samurai, who accounted for less than 10 percent of the population, were made a closed caste as part of a larger effort to freeze the social order and stabilize society. Most samurai were forced to become civil bureaucrats or take up some trade during the 250 years of peace that prevailed under the Tokugawa shogunate. In spite of their high social rank, a growing number of samurai families suffered impoverishment by the end of this period.

Lower-ranking samurai took part in the movement against the Tokugawa regime that resulted in the Meiji Restoration of 1868. The samurai class lost its privileged position when feudalism was officially abolished in 1871. Discontented former samurai rose in rebellion several times during the 1870s, but these revolts were quickly suppressed by the newly established national army.

as agricultural practices advanced; other aspects of society were changing as well. Artisans were frequently attached to the proprietors of the *shōen* and progressively became more specialized, responding to a specific growth of consumer demand. Centres for metal casting and metalworking, paper manufacture, and other skills appeared outside the capital, in various provincial localities, for the first time. The exchange of agricultural products, manufactured goods, and other products thrived; local markets, held on three fixed days a month, became common. Copper coins from Sung China circulated in these markets, while itinerant merchants increased their activity. Bills of exchange were also used for payments to distant localities. In the large ports along the Inland Sea and Lake Biwa, specialized wholesale merchants (*toimaru*) appeared who, as contractors, stored, transported, and sold goods. Further, it became common for many merchants and artisans to form guilds, known as *za*, organized under the temples, shrines, or civil aristocrats, from whom they gained special monopoly privileges and exemptions from customs duties.

The Oda Regime

In the 1550–60 period the Sengoku *daimyo*, who had survived the wars of the previous 100 years, moved into an even fiercer stage of mutual conflict. These powerful *daimyo* were harassed not only by each other but also by the rise of common people within their domains. The *daimyo* sought to resolve their dilemma by acquiring land and people to widen their domains and, finally, by trying to seize control of the whole country. That, of course, required the control of Kyōto, the political centre of Japan since ancient times. Out of these bloody struggles emerged one Sengoku *daimyo*, Oda Nobunaga of Owari province, who succeeded in occupying the capital as the first feudal unifier.

The emergence of Nobunaga's regime reversed the feudal disintegration of the previous century and moved the country toward unification. Oda was a military genius, who was the first to successfully adapt firearms to Japanese warfare. His bold wars of suppression, waged against both other *daimyo* and recalcitrant religious communities, led to a great redrawing of the political map of Japan, previously split up among *daimyo* throughout the country. In the Kinai district, where Nobunaga's conquered territory was centred, however, he established control by dividing his new domain among his commanders. Rather than completely abrogating the long-established privileges of the temples, shrines, and local landlords (*kokujin*), he at first recognized them, regarding them as an important adjunct to the strengthening of his military power and using them as followers in his battles for unification. Cadastral surveys aimed at strengthening feudal landownership were at this stage carried out not so much to gain control over the complicated landholding and taxation system of the farmers as to define the size of fiefs (*chigyō*) of Nobunaga's retainers in order to confirm the extent of their military services and obligations to him.

Nobunaga's unification policy was predicated on a separation of warriors from the farmers, but unification was hampered because of resistance from old political forces, especially several major Buddhist temples. Unification proceeded further during the era of Nobunaga's successor, Toyotomi Hideyoshi.

The Weakening of the *Bakuhan* System

As Japan entered the 18th century, the *bakuhan* system began to show signs of weakness. The finances of both the *bakufu* and the *han* were theoretically based on a rice-producing economy, in which administrators endeavoured to levy taxes to be paid in kind, mostly in rice, centred on the annual crop. Rice and other crops were then transported to the great central cities of Edo and Ōsaka, where they were exchanged for money. The extremely diverse economic and social life of these cities was based upon a money economy in which people and produce were constantly exchanged. This activity radiated outward to the various *daimyo* castle towns and, inevitably, into the countryside as well. Thus, even the rural areas of Japan were increasingly drawn into a monetized economy, and peasants everywhere paid part of their taxes in money. If commercial development had been largely a phenomenon of the cities in the 17th century, in the 18th and 19th centuries it spread to the hinterlands of Japan, where small-scale producers of goods, distributors, and even retailers appeared. Inevitably, it meant the rise of some wealthy members of the rural populace, who used their wealth to invest in land and commercial ventures and to "ape their betters" in the cities in both custom and culture. Few farmers, however, prospered through producing commercial goods, and the majority of peasants remained impoverished. Rural villages were characterized by a few wealthy farmers, a majority of small-scale independent landholders, and a growing number of impoverished tenants. Many small-scale farmers, squeezed by the demands of commercial development, were forced to part with their lands and fell into tenancy.

Thus, as the commercial economy extended into rural villages, social divisions arose among the farmers. Tax collection became unstable, and many warriors—whose stipends, still calculated in *koku*, depended upon taxes paid by the farmers—found themselves in serious financial difficulty. Despite the general improvement of agricultural technology and the spread of such knowledge through manuals and handbooks among an increasingly literate populace during the Edo period, productivity was uneven; and in many areas, and especially during certain eras, periodic crop failures and famines, exacerbated by excessive taxation, resulted in people starving or fleeing their villages. The abandonment of cultivated land also became conspicuous. As noted above, the samurai class had long since taken up normal residence in the cities. With the development of the urban way of life, they now incurred increasing expenses, despite a spate of *bakufu* and domain exhortations to practice frugality. Living on fixed incomes, many became greatly impoverished. At times, both the *bakufu* and the domains tried to suppress commercial production as a means of alleviating the suffering of their vassals; but this met with great resistance from merchants and affected the self-sufficient economy of the farmers as well. It was, in any event, a hopeless effort, given the scale of commercial development nationwide. When attempts to restrict production failed, *bakufu* and *han* administrators encouraged such production, seeking to supplement their finances by monopolizing the farmers' commercial goods and selling them themselves. Thus, on top of excessive taxes, farmers also were sometimes deprived of the profits of their commercial goods.

Ultimately, such rural conditions led to major outbreaks of violence. Stratification of rural villages—a growing gap between wealthy and poor farmers—tenancy, the inability of many to survive the harsh realities of commercialization, and exploitation by feudal lords forced some peasants into uprisings (*hyakushō ikki*). Even in early Edo times, there were localized demonstrations against *daimyo* for excessive taxation, but from the 18th century peasant protest became increasingly violent and widespread. Some uprisings were directed at local lords, some were more widespread, and some were directed not at feudal warrior overlords but at wealthy peasant landlords and village headmen who also had become exploitative. Meanwhile, economic conditions in the cities—to which frustrated peasants often fled seeking a better life—were hardly better. While many wealthy merchants enjoyed luxurious lifestyles in cooperation with warrior rulers, the city poor, driven to the edge of starvation by the rising prices of rice and other commodities, often rioted, plundering and destroying rice shops and pawnshops.

Abolition of Feudalism

The Meiji reformers began with measures that addressed the decentralized feudal structure to which they attributed Japan's weakness. In 1869 the lords of Satsuma, Chōshū, Tosa, and Saga were persuaded to return their lands to the throne. Others quickly followed suit. The court took steps to standardize the administration of the domains, appointing their former *daimyo* as governors. In 1871 the governor-*daimyo* were summoned to Tokyo and told that the domains were officially abolished. The 250 former domains now became 72 prefectures and three metropolitan districts, a number later reduced by one-third. In the process, most *daimyo* were eased out of administrative roles, and though rewarded with titles in a new European-style peerage in 1884, were effectively removed from political power.

The Meiji leaders also realized that they had to end the complex class system that had existed under feudalism. Yet, it was difficult to deal with the samurai, who numbered, with dependents, almost two million in 1868. Starting in 1869 the old hierarchy was replaced by a simpler division that established three orders: court nobles and former feudal lords became *kazoku* ("peers"); former samurai, *shizoku*, and all others (including outcast groups) now became *heimin* ("commoners"). The samurai were initially given annual pensions, but financial duress forced the conversion of these into lump-sum payments of interest-bearing but nonconvertible bonds in 1876. Other symbolic class distinctions such as the hairstyle of samurai and the privilege of wearing swords were abolished.

Many former samurai lacked commercial experience and squandered their bonds. Inflation also undercut their value. A national conscription system instituted in 1873 further deprived samurai of their monopoly on military service.

Samurai discontent resulted in numerous revolts, the most serious occurring in the southwest, where the restoration movement had started and warriors expected the greatest rewards. An uprising in Chōshū expressed dissatisfaction with administrative measures that deprived the samurai of their status and income. In Saga, samurai called for a foreign war to provide employment for their class. The last, and by far the greatest, revolt came in Satsuma in 1877. This rebellion was led by the restoration hero Saigō Takamori and lasted six months. The imperial government's conscript levies were hard-pressed to defeat Saigō, but in the end superior transport, modern communications, and better weapons assured victory for the government. In this, as in the other revolts, issues were localized, and the loyalties of most Satsuma men in the central government remained with the imperial cause.

Land surveys were begun in 1873 to determine the amount and value of land based on average rice yields in recent years, and a monetary tax of 3 percent of land value was established. The same surveys led to certificates of land ownership for farmers, who were released from feudal controls. The land measures involved basic changes, and there was widespread confusion and uncertainty among farmers that expressed itself in the form of short-lived revolts and demonstrations. But the establishment of private ownership, and measures to promote new technology, fertilizers, and seeds, produced a rise in agricultural output. The land tax, supplemented by printed money, became the principal source of government revenue for several decades.

Although it was hard-pressed for money, the government initiated a program of industrialization, which was seen as essential for national strength. Except for military industries and strategic communications, this program was largely in private hands, although the government set up pilot plants to provide encouragement. Trade and manufacturing benefited from a growing national market and legal security, but the unequal treaties enacted with foreign powers made it impossible to protect industries with tariffs until 1911.

In the 1880s fear of excessive inflation led the government to sell its remaining plants to private investors—usually individuals with close ties to those in power. As a result, a small group of men came to dominate many industries. Collectively they became known as the *zaibatsu*, or financial cliques. With great opportunities and few competitors, *zaibatsu* firms came to dominate enterprise after enterprise. Sharing a similar vision for the country, these men maintained close ties to the government leadership. The House of Mitsui, for instance, was on friendly terms with many of the Meiji oligarchs, and that of Mitsubishi was founded by a Tosa samurai who had been an associate of those within the government's inner circle.

Equally important for building a modern state was the development of national identity. True national unity required the propagation of new loyalties among the general populace and the transformation of powerless and inarticulate peasants into citizens of a centralized state. The use of religion and ideology was vital to this process. Early Meiji policy, therefore, elevated Shintō to the highest position in the new religious hierarchy, replacing Buddhism with a cult of national deities that supported the throne. Christianity was reluctantly legalized in 1873, but, while important for some intellectuals, it was treated with suspicion by many in the government. The challenge remained how to use traditional values without risking foreign condemnation that the government was forcing a state religion upon the Japanese. By the 1890s the education system provided the ideal vehicle to inculcate the new ideological orientation. A system of universal education had been announced in 1872. For a time its organization and philosophy were Western, but during the 1880s a new emphasis on ethics emerged as the government tried to counter excessive Westernization and followed European ideas on nationalist education. In 1890 the Imperial Rescript on Education (Kyōiku Chokugo) laid out the lines of Confucian and Shintō ideology, which constituted the moral content of later Japanese education. Thus, loyalty to the emperor, who was hedged about with Confucian teachings and Shintō reverence, became the centre of a citizen's ideology. To avoid charges of indoctrination, the state distinguished between this secular cult and actual religion, permitting "religious freedom" while requiring a form of worship as the patriotic duty of all Japanese. The education system also was used to project into the citizenry at large the ideal of samurai loyalty that had been the heritage of the ruling class.

India and the Caste System

There is considerable controversy among historians as to whether it would be accurate to describe India's feudatory pattern as feudalism per se. Some argue that, although it was not identical to the classic example of feudalism in western Europe, there are sufficient similarities to allow the use of the term. Others contend that the dissimilarities are substantial, such as the apparent absence of an economic contract involving king, vassal, and serf. In any event, the patterns of land relations, politics, and culture changed considerably, and the major characteristic of the change consists of forms of decentralization.

The commonly used term for a feudatory was *samanta*, which designated either a conquered ruler or a secular official connected with the administration who had been given a grant of land in lieu of a salary and who had asserted ownership over the land and gradually appropriated rights of ruling the area. There were various categories of *samantas*. As long as a ruler was in a feudatory status, he called himself *samanta* and acknowledged his overlord in official documents and charters. Independent status was indicated by the elimination of the title of *samanta* and the inclusion instead of royal titles such as *maharaja* and *maharatadhiraja*. The feudatory had certain obligations to the ruler. Although virtually in sole control administratively and fiscally over the land granted to him, he nevertheless had to pay a small percentage of the revenue to the ruler and maintain a specified body of troops for him. He was permitted the use of certain symbols of authority on formal occasions and was required, if called upon, to give his daughter in marriage to his suzerain. These major administrative and economic changes, although primarily concerning fiscal arrangements and revenue organization, also had their impact on politics and culture. The grantees or intermediaries in a hierarchy of grants were not merely secular officials but were often Brahman beneficiaries who had been given grants of land in return for religious services rendered to the state. The grants were frequently so lucrative that the Brahmans could marry into the families of local chiefs, which explains the presence of Brahman ancestors in the genealogies of the period.

The Hindu Caste System

The caste system is any of the ranked, hereditary, endogamous social groups, often linked with occupation, that together constitute traditional societies in South Asia, particularly among Hindus in India. Although sometimes used to designate similar groups in other societies, the caste system is uniquely developed in Hindu societies.

The History of Castes

Use of the term "caste" to characterize social organization in South Asia, particularly among the Hindus, dates to the middle of the 16th century. *Casta* (from Latin *castus*, "chaste") in the sense of purity of breed was employed by Portuguese observers to describe the division of Hindu society in western and southwestern India into socially ranked occupational categories. In an effort to maintain vertical social distance, these groups practiced mutual exclusion in matters relating to eating and, presumably, marrying. Subsequently, cast, or caste, became established in English and major European languages (notably Dutch and French) in the same specific sense. Caste is generally believed to be an ancient, abiding, and unique Indian institution upheld by a complex cultural ideology.

Varnas

It is essential to distinguish between large-scale and small-scale views of caste society, which may respectively be said to represent theory and practice, or ideology and the existing social reality. On the large scale, contemporary students of Hindu society recall an ancient fourfold arrangement of socioeconomic categories called the *varnas*, which is traced back to an oral tradition preserved in the *Rigveda* (dating perhaps from between 1500 and 1200 BCE). The Sanskrit word *varna* has many connotations, including colour, description, selection, and classification.

Indo-European-speaking peoples migrated probably about 1500 BCE to northwestern India (the Indus valley and the Punjab Plain). Since the mid-19th century some scholars have identified these migrants as "Aryans"; this term, derived from the Sanskrit word *arya* ("noble" or "distinguished"), is found in the *Rigveda*. Some scholars postulated that these alleged Aryans encountered or conquered the indigenous people, whom they called *daha* ("enemies") or *dasyu* ("servants"). The fact that *varna* may mean "colour" has led some scholars to posit that these so-called Aryans and the *dasyus*—alleged to have been light-skinned and dark-skinned, respectively—may have been antagonistic ethnic groups divided by physical features as well as by culture and language. Since the mid-20th century, however, some scholars have pointed to textual evidence that the distinction referred to ritual practices and not to skin colour; further, the term *arya* may have been a term for nobility rather than an ethnic self-identification. In addition, it is also likely that the *daha* included earlier immigrants from Iran. Therefore, the tendency of some 20th-century writers to reduce the ancient bipolar classification to racial differences on the basis of skin colour is misleading and rightly no longer in vogue.

Whatever the relations between the so-called *arya* and *daha*, it is likely that they gradually became integrated into an internally plural social order reflecting a threefold division of society into priests, warriors, and commoners. In an early period, membership in a *varna* appears to have been based mainly on personal skills rather than birth, status, or wealth. By the end of the Rigvedic period, however, the hereditary principle of social rank had taken root. Thus the hymn of the *Rigveda* (probably a late addition to the text) in which the creation of humanity in the form of *varnas* emerges from a self-sacrificial rite of the primeval person (*purusha*): Brahmans were the mouth of *purusha*, from his arms were made the Rajanyas (Kshatriyas), from his two thighs, the Vaishyas, and the Shudras were born from his feet. The extent to which the ideology's hierarchical ordering of the four groups mirrored the social reality is unknown.

The highest-ranked among the *varnas*, the Brahmans, were priests and the masters and teachers of sacred knowledge (*veda*). Next in rank but hardly socially inferior was the ruling class of Rajanya (kinsmen of the king), later renamed Kshatriya, those endowed with sovereignty and, as warriors, responsible for the protection of the dominion (*kshatra*). A complex, mutually reinforcing relationship of sacerdotal authority and temporal power was obviously shaped over a long period of time.

A Brahman priest with holy fire offering a blessing at a temple in India. The priestly Brahman social class is made up of the highest-ranked castes. EyesWideOpen/ Getty Images

Clearly ranked below the two top categories were the Vaishyas (from *vish*, "those settled on soils"), comprising agriculturists and merchants. These three *varnas* together were deemed to be "twice-born" (*dvija*), as the male members were entitled to go through a rite of initiation during childhood. This second birth entitled them to participate in specified sacraments and gave them access to sacred knowledge. They were also entitled alongside their social superiors to demand and receive menial services from the Shudras, the fourth and lowest-ranked *varna*. Certain degrading occupations, such as disposal of dead animals, excluded some Shudras from any physical contact with the "twice-born" varnas.

Women search through a garbage pile for items of worth in Kolkata, India. In Hindu society, demeaning tasks such as this are generally left to the lower castes. Frank Bienewald/LightRocket/Getty Images

Considered untouchable, they were simply dubbed "the fifth" (*panchama*) category.

In the *varna* framework, the Brahmans have everything, directly or indirectly: "noble" identity, "twice-born" status, sacerdotal authority, and dominion over the Vaishyas and the Shudras, who accounted for the great majority of the people. This is not surprising, for the ancient Brahmans were the authors of the ideology. The four *varnas*, together with the notional division of the individual life cycle into four stages, or *ashramas* (*brahmacharya*, the years of learning and extreme discipline; *garhasthya*, householdership; *vanaprastha*, retirement; and *sannyasa*, renunciation of all worldly bonds) may at best be considered an archetypical blueprint for the good, moral life. Indeed, the Hindu way of life is traditionally called the *varnashrama dharma* (duties of the stages of life for one's *varna*). The *varna* order remains relevant to the understanding of the system of *jatis*, as it provides the ideological setting for the patterns of interaction that are continuously under negotiation.

CHAPTER 6

CLASS DISTINCTION AND LAND RIGHTS IN THE OTTOMAN EMPIRE

During the 16th century the institutions of society and government that had been evolving in the Ottoman dominions for two centuries reached the classical forms and patterns that were to persist into modern times. The basic division in Ottoman society was the traditional Middle Eastern distinction between a small ruling class of Ottomans (Osmanlı) and a large mass of subjects called *rayas* (*re'âyâ*). Three attributes were essential for membership in the Ottoman ruling class: profession of loyalty to the sultan and his state; acceptance and practice of Islām and its underlying system of thought and action; and knowledge and practice of the complicated system of customs, behaviour, and language known as the Ottoman Way. Those who lacked any of these attributes were considered to be members of the subject class, the "protected flock" of the sultan.

Classical Ottoman Society and Administration

Social mobility was based on the possession of these definable and attainable attributes. *Rayas* able to acquire them could rise into the ruling class, and Ottomans who came to lack any of them became members of the subject class. Members of the ruling class were considered the sultan's slaves and

Sultan

Originally, according to the Qur'ān, a sultan (Arabic *Sulṭān*) was considered a moral or spiritual authority. The term later came to denote political or governmental power and from the 11th century was used as a title by Muslim sovereigns.

Maḥmūd of Ghazna (reigned 998–1030 CE) was the first Muslim ruler to be called sultan by his contemporaries, and under the Seljuqs of Anatolia and Iran it became a regular title. Thereafter it was frequently conferred on sovereigns by the caliph (titular head of the Muslim community) and came to be used throughout the Islāmic world.

acquired their master's social status. As slaves, however, their properties, lives, and persons were entirely at his disposition. Their basic functions were to preserve the Islāmic nature of the state and to rule and defend the empire. By Ottoman theory the main attribute of the sultan's sovereignty was the right to possess and exploit all sources of wealth in the empire. The function of enlarging, protecting, and exploiting that wealth for the benefit of the sultan and his state, therefore, was the main duty of the ruling class. The *rayas* produced the wealth by farming the land or engaging in trade and industry and then paying a portion of the resulting profits to the ruling class in the form of taxes.

Organizations and hierarchies were developed by the ruling and subject classes to carry out their functions in Ottoman society. The ruling class divided itself into four functional institutions: the imperial, or palace (*mülkiye*), institution, personally led by the sultan, which provided the leadership and direction for the other institutions as well as for the entire Ottoman system; the military (*seyfiye* or *askeriye*) institution, which was responsible for expanding and defending the empire and keeping order and security within the sultan's dominions; the administrative, or scribal (*kalemiye*), institution, organized as the imperial treasury (*hazine-i amire*), which was in charge of collecting and spending the imperial revenues; and the religious, or cultural (*ilmiye*), institution, comprising the *ulama* (Muslims expert in the religious sciences), which was in charge of organizing and propagating the faith and maintaining and enforcing the religious law (Sharī'ah or Şeriat)— its interpretation in the courts, its expounding in the mosques and schools, and its study and interpretation.

A manuscript illustration showing Turkish troops preparing for battle against the Hungarians in 1526. The military was part of the Ottoman ruling class. De Agostini/ Getty Images

Organization of the Ottoman Subject Class

To cover the areas of life not included within the scope of the ruling class of Ottomans, members of the subject class were allowed to organize themselves as they wished. As a natural manifestation of Middle Eastern society, their organization was determined largely by religious and occupational distinctions. The basic class divisions within the subject class were determined by religion, with each important group organizing into a relatively self-contained autonomous community usually called a millet (also *taife* or *cemaat*), which operated under its own laws and customs and was directed by a religious leader responsible to the sultan for the fulfillment of the duties and responsibilities of the millet members, particularly those of paying taxes and security. In addition, each millet cared for the many social and administrative functions not assumed by the Ottoman ruling class, concerning such matters as marriage, divorce, birth and death, health, education, internal security, and justice. Within the millets, just as in Ottoman society as a whole, there was social mobility, with people moving up and down the ladder according to ability and luck. Individuals could pass from one millet to another if they wished to convert, but, because all the millets were extremely antagonistic toward those who left them to convert to another religion, the state discouraged such action as much as possible to preserve social harmony and tranquility.

The purpose of the millet system was to keep the different peoples of the empire separated in order to minimize conflict and preserve social order in a highly heterogeneous state. Christian hatred of Muslims and Jews, however, led to constant tension and competition among the different millets, with the Jews being subjected to "blood libel" attacks against their persons, shops, and homes by the sultan's Greek and Armenian subjects. These attacks intensified during the week preceding Easter, when Greeks and Armenians were driven into a frenzy by the old accusations, invented in ancient times by the Greek Orthodox church, that Jews murdered Christian children in order to use their blood for religious rituals. The sultan intervened to provide protection for his

Jewish subjects as much as possible, though the fact that many of his soldiers were converted Christians who retained the hatreds instilled in their childhoods made this intervention very difficult.

In addition to the religion-based millets, Ottoman subjects also organized themselves by economic function into guilds. These guilds regulated economic activities, setting quality and pricing standards that guild members had to maintain in order to continue in their occupations. In most cases particular occupations were monopolized by members of one millet, but, in some trades practiced by members of different religions, guild membership cut across religious boundaries, joining members of different religions in common organizations based not on class, rank, or religion but on mutually shared values and beliefs, economic activities, and social needs. Through contact and cooperation in such guilds, members of the different groups of Ottoman society were cemented into a common whole, performing many of the social and economic functions outside the scope of the ruling class and the millets, particularly those functions associated with economic regulation and social security. In many cases guilds also were associated intimately with mystic religious orders, which—providing a more personal religious experience than that provided by the established Muslim and non-Muslim religious organizations—came to dominate Ottoman society in its centuries of decline.

Sources of Revenue

Within the Ottoman ruling class the most important unit of organization and action was the *mukâṭaʿa*, in which a member of the ruling class was given a portion of the sultan's revenues along with authority to use the revenues for purposes determined by the sultan. The exact nature of the *mukâṭaʿa* depended on the proportion of the revenues that the holder remitted to the treasury and the proportion he retained for himself. Three types of *mukâṭaʿa* were found: *timars, emanets,* and *iltizāms.*

The *timar,* traditionally described as a fief, only superficially resembled European feudalism; it was part of a centralized system and did not involve the mutual rights and obligations that characterized feudalism in the West. In return for services to the state, the *timar* holder was given the full profits of the source of revenue for his personal exploitation and profit; these profits were independent of, and in addition to, those connected with the exploitation of the *timar* itself. For many military and administrative positions *timars* normally were given in lieu of salaries, thus relieving the treasury of the trouble and expense of collecting revenues and disbursing them to its employees as salaries. Almost all of the 14th- and 15th-century Ottoman conquests in southeastern Europe were distributed as *timars* to military officers, who in return assumed administrative responsibility in peacetime and provided soldiers and military leadership for the Ottoman army in war. Many of the officers of the central government also were rewarded with *timars* in place of, or in addition to, salaries paid by the treasury.

A less common form of the *mukâṭaʿa* was the *emanet* ("trusteeship"), held by the *emin* ("trustee" or "agent"). In contrast to the *timar* holder, the *emin* turned all his proceeds over to the treasury and was compensated entirely by salary, thus being the closest Ottoman equivalent to the modern government official. The legal rationale for this arrangement was that the *emin* undertook no additional service beyond administering the *mukâṭaʿa* and thus had no right to share in its profits. Used primarily for urban custom houses and market police, *emanets* were closely supervised by the central government and its agents and did not need the profit motive in order to assure efficiency on the part of the holders.

The most common kind of *mukâta'a*, and therefore the most prevalent type of administrative unit in the Ottoman system, was the tax farm (*iltizām*), which combined elements of both the *timar* and *emanet*. As in the *timar*, the tax farmer (*mültezim*) could keep only a part of the tax he collected and had to deliver the balance to the treasury. This was because his service consisted only of his work in administering the *mukâta'a*, for which he was given a share of his collection instead of the *emin*'s salary. The tax farmer thus was given the inducement of profit to be as efficient as possible. Most of Anatolia and the Arab provinces were administered in this way because they were conquered at a time when the government's

The Ottoman Cavalry

The status of the *sipahi* (from Persian for "cavalryman") of the Ottoman Empire resembled that of the medieval European knight. He was a holder of a fief, known as a *timar*, that was granted directly by the Ottoman sultan, and was entitled to all of the income from it in return for military service. The peasants on the land were subsequently attached to the land and became serfs.

Sipahis provided the bulk of the Ottoman army until about the mid-16th century. From then on they were gradually supplanted by the Janissaries, an elite corps composed of infantrymen paid regular salaries by the sultanate. In part, this change resulted from the increased use of firearms, which made cavalry less important, and from the need to maintain a regular standing army. The *sipahis* were completely discredited during the war of Greek independence (1821–32).

need for cash to pay the salaried Janissary infantry and supply an increasingly lavish court required the treasury to seek out all the revenues it could find. As the *timar*-based *sipahi* cavalry became less important and as the Turkish notables who held most of the *timars* lost most of their political power during the time of Süleyman, the estates gradually fell into the hands of the *devşirme* class. *Devşirme* was the term used to describe the practice by Ottoman sultans of choosing young Christian boys from the conquered states, converting them to Islam, and pressing them into service as soldiers.

Ottoman Religious and Civil Law

The legal and customary bases of organization and action in Ottoman society depended on a dual system of law: the Sharī'ah, or Muslim religious law, and the *kanun*, or civil law. The Sharī'ah was the basic law of Ottoman society, as it was of all Muslim communities. Considered to be a divinely inspired corpus of political, social, and moral regulations and principles, the Sharī'ah was intended to cover all aspects of life for Muslims, although it was highly developed only in the issues of personal behaviour that affected the early Muslim community and were reflected in the Qur'ān and early Muslim tradition. It never was developed in detail in matters of public law, state organization, and administration. Its general principles left room for interpretation and legislation on specific matters by secular authorities, and the Muslim judges of the Ottoman Empire recognized the right of the sultan to legislate in civil laws as long as he did not conflict with the Sharī'ah in detail or principle.

The Sharī'ah, therefore, provided the principles of public law and covered matters of personal behaviour and status in the Muslim millets in the same way that the members of the Christian and Jewish millets were subject to their own religious codes. The Sharī'ah was interpreted and enforced by members of the cultural institution, the *ulama*, just as the laws of each non-Muslim millet were enforced by its leaders. The members of the *ulama* who interpreted the law in the courts, called *qadis*, as well as the jurisconsults, called *muftis*, had the right to invalidate any secular law they felt contradicted the Sharī'ah; however, they rarely used this right, because as part of the ruling class they were under the authority of the sultan and could be removed from their positions. The sultan therefore was relatively free to issue secular laws to meet the needs of the time, a major factor in the long survival of the empire. It must be noted, however, that, with the restricted scope of the Ottoman ruling class and state and the large areas of power and function left to the religious communities, guilds, and Ottoman officials who held the *mukâṭa'a*, the sultans were never as autocratic as has been assumed. It was only in the 19th century that Ottoman reformers centralized government and society on Western lines and restricted or ended the traditional autonomies that had done so much to decentralize power in the previous centuries.

Internal Problems

The reign of Süleyman I the Magnificent marked the peak of Ottoman grandeur, but signs of weakness signaled the beginning of a slow but steady decline. An important factor in the decline was the increasing lack of ability and power of the sultans themselves. Süleyman tired of the campaigns and arduous duties of administration and withdrew more and more from public affairs to devote himself to the pleasures of his harem. To take his place, the office of grand vizier was built up to become second only to the sultan in authority and revenue; the grand vizier's authority included the right to demand and obtain absolute obedience. But, while the grand vizier

Portrait of Süleyman I, during whose reign the Ottoman Empire reached its apex but also saw the timar *start to falter.* Leemage/Universal Images Group/Getty Images

was able to stand in for the sultan in official functions, he could not take his place as the focus of loyalty for all the different classes and groups in the empire. The resulting separation of political loyalty and central authority led to a decline in the government's ability to impose its will.

The mid-16th century also saw the triumph of the *devşirme* over the Turkish nobility, which lost almost all its power and position in the capital and returned to its old centres of power in southeastern Europe and Anatolia. In consequence, many of the *timars* formerly assigned to the notables to support the *sipahi* cavalry were seized by the *devşirme* and transformed into great estates—becoming, for all practical purposes, private property—thus depriving the state of their services as well as the revenue they could have produced if they had been transformed into tax farms. While the *sipahis* did not entirely disappear as a military force, the Janissaries and the associated artillery corps became the most important segments of the Ottoman army.

Corruption and Nepotism

Because the sultans no longer could control the *devşirme* by setting it against the Turkish notables, the *devşirme* gained control of the sultans and used the government for its own benefit rather than for the benefit of a sultan or his empire. In consequence, corruption and nepotism took hold at all levels of administration. In addition, with the challenge of the notables gone, the *devşirme* class itself broke into countless factions and parties, each working for its own advantage by supporting the candidacy of a particular imperial prince and forming close alliances with corresponding palace factions led by the mothers, sisters, and wives of each prince. After Süleyman, therefore, accession and appointments to positions came less as the result of ability than as a consequence of the political maneuverings of the *devşirme*-harem political parties. Those in power found it more convenient to control the princes by keeping them uneducated and inexperienced, and the old tradition by which young princes were educated in the field was replaced by a system in which all the princes were isolated in the private apartments of the harem and limited to such education as its permanent inhabitants could provide. In consequence, few of the sultans after Süleyman had the ability to exercise real power, even when circumstances might have given them the opportunity. But the lack of ability did not affect the sultans' desire for power; lacking the means developed by their predecessors to achieve this end, they developed new ones. Selim II (ruled 1566–74), known as "the Sot" or "the Blonde," and Murad III (1574–95) both gained power by playing off the different factions and by weakening the office of grand vizier, the main administrative vehicle for factional and party influence in the declining Ottoman state. As the grand viziers lost their dominant position following the downfall of Mehmed Sokollu (served 1565–79), power fell first into the hands of the women of the harem, during the "Sultanate of the Women" (1570–78), and then into the grasp of the chief Janissary officers, the agas, who dominated from 1578 to 1625. No matter who controlled the apparatus of government during this time, however, the results were the same—a growing paralysis of administration throughout the empire, increasing anarchy and misrule, and the fracture of society into discrete and increasingly hostile communities.

Economic Difficulties

Under such conditions it was inevitable that the Ottoman government could not meet the increasingly difficult problems that plagued the empire in the 16th and 17th centuries. Economic difficulties began in the late 16th century, when the Dutch and British completely closed the old international trade routes through the Middle East. As a result the prosperity of the Middle Eastern provinces declined. The Ottoman economy was disrupted by inflation, caused by the influx of precious metals into Europe from the Americas and by an increasing imbalance of trade between East and West. As the treasury lost more of its revenues to the depredations of the *devşirme*, it began to meet its obligations by debasing the coinage, sharply increasing taxes, and resorting to confiscations, all of which only worsened the situation. All those depending on salaries found themselves underpaid, resulting in further theft, overtaxation, and corruption. Holders of the *timars* and tax farms started using them as sources of revenue to be exploited as rapidly as possible, rather than as long-term holdings whose prosperity had to be maintained to provide for the future. Political influence and corruption also enabled them to transform these holdings into private property, either as life holdings (*malikâne*) or religious endowments (*vakif*), without any further obligations to the state.

Inflation also weakened the traditional industries and trades. Functioning under strict price regulations, the guilds were unable to provide quality goods at prices low enough to compete with the cheap European manufactured goods that entered the empire without restriction because of the Capitulations agreements. In consequence, traditional Ottoman industry fell into rapid decline. Christian subjects combined with foreign diplomats and merchants, who were protected by the Capitulations, largely to drive the sultan's Muslim and Jewish subjects out of industry and commerce and into poverty and despair.

Social Unrest

These conditions were exacerbated by large population growth during the 16th and 17th centuries, part of the general population rise that occurred in much of Europe at this time. The amount of subsistence available not only failed to expand to meet the needs of the rising population but in fact fell as the result of the anarchic political and economic conditions. Social distress increased and disorder resulted. Landless and jobless peasants fled off the land, as did cultivators subjected to confiscatory taxation at the hands of *timariots* and tax farmers, thus reducing food supplies even more. Many peasants fled to the cities, exacerbating the food shortage, and reacted against their troubles by rising against the established order; many more remained in the countryside and joined rebel bands, known as *levends* and Jelālīs (Celâlis), which took what they could from those who remained to cultivate and trade.

The central government became weaker, and as more peasants joined rebel bands they were able to take over large parts of the empire, keeping all the remaining tax revenues for themselves and often cutting off the regular food supplies to the cities and the Ottoman armies still guarding the frontiers. Under such conditions the armies broke up, with most of the salaried positions in the Janissary and other corps becoming no more than new sources of revenue, without their holders performing any military services in return. Thus, the Ottoman armies came to be composed primarily of fighting contingents supplied by the vassals of the sultan, particularly the Crimean Tartar khans, together with whatever rabble could be dragged from the streets of the cities whenever required by campaigns. The Ottoman army still remained strong enough to curb the most pressing provincial revolts, but the revolts proliferated through the centuries of decline, making effective administration almost impossible outside the major cities still under the government's control. In many ways the substratum of Ottoman society—formed by the millets and various economic, social, and religious guilds and buttressed by the organization of the Ottoman *ulama*— cushioned the mass of the people and the ruling class itself from the worst effects of this multisided disintegration and enabled the empire to survive much longer than otherwise would have been possible.

External Relations

Despite these difficulties, the internal Ottoman weakness was evident to only the most discerning Ottoman and foreign observers during much of the 17th century. Most Europeans continued to fear the Ottoman army as they had two centuries earlier, and, although its ability was reduced, it remained strong enough to prevent the provincial rebels from assuming complete control and even to make a few more significant conquests in both East and West. The empire suffered defeats for the first time, but it retained reserve strength sufficient for it to recoup when needed and to prevent the loss of any integral parts of the empire. Although the Ottoman navy was destroyed by the fleet of the Holy League at the Battle of Lepanto (1571), it was able to rebuild and regain naval mastery in the eastern Mediterranean through the rest of the 16th and most of the 17th century, taking Tunis from the Spanish Habsburgs (1574), Fez from the Portuguese (1578), and Crete from Venice (1669). In consequence, as long as Europe continued to fear the Ottomans, no one tried to upset the precarious peace treaties concluded in Süleyman's later years, and the Ottomans were shielded from their own weakness for quite some time. Despite the upsets then disturbing the body politic, the Ottomans occasionally undertook new campaigns. When the rising principality of Moscow conquered the last Mongol states in Central Asia and reached the Caspian Sea, thus posing a threat to the Ottoman positions north of the Black Sea and in the Caucasus, Murad III conquered the northern sections of the Caucasus and, taking advantage of the anarchy in Iran that followed the death of Shah Ṭahmāsp I in 1576, seized long-coveted Azerbaijan. He thus brought the empire to the peak of its territorial extent and added wealthy new provinces whose revenues, for a half century at least, rescued the Ottoman treasury from the worst of its financial troubles and gave the empire a respite during which it could attempt to remedy its worst problems.

Reform Efforts

The Ottoman reforms introduced during the 17th century were undertaken by sultans Osman II (ruled 1618–22) and Murad IV (1623–40) and by the famous dynasty of Köprülü grand viziers who served under Mehmed IV (1648–87)—Köprülü Mehmed Paşa (served 1656–61) and Köprülü Fazıl Ahmed Paşa (served 1661–76). Each of these early reformers rose as the result of crises and military defeats that threatened the very existence of the empire. Each was given the power needed to introduce reforms because of the fears of the ruling class that the empire, on which the privileges of the ruling class depended, was in mortal danger. In a war between the Ottomans and the Habsburgs that began in 1593, the Austrians were able to take much of central Hungary and Romania, and only an accidental Ottoman triumph in 1596 enabled the sultan to recoup. The Habsburgs then agreed to the Treaty of Zsitvatorok (1606), by which Ottoman rule of Hungary and Romania was restored. The treaty itself, however, like the events that led up to it, for the first time demonstrated to

Europe the extent of Ottoman weakness and thus exposed the Ottomans to new dangers in subsequent years.

In the East, anarchy in Iran was brought to an end by Shah 'Abbās I, who not only restored Iranian power but also conquered Iraq (1624) and threatened to take the entire Ottoman Empire. Though Murad IV was able to retake Iraq (1638), Iran remained a major threat. Finally, a long war with Venice (1645–69), occasioned by Ottoman efforts to capture Crete, exposed Istanbul to a major Venetian naval attack. Although the Venetians finally were pushed back in a naval campaign culminating in the Ottoman conquest of Crete (1669), they still posed a major threat that, like those which had occurred earlier in the century, stimulated the ruling class to accept needed reforms. The reforms introduced during the 17th century were too limited in nature and scope, however, to permanently arrest the Ottoman decline. The reforms essentially were no more than efforts to restore the inherited system of government and society that had operated successfully in the past. Efforts were made to restore the *timar* and tax farm systems as the basis of the administration and army and to limit taxes to the limits imposed by law. Provincial revolts were suppressed, peasants were forced back to the land, and cultivation was increased. Debased coins were replaced by coins of full value. Industry and trade were encouraged, corrupt officials executed, and insubordination driven out.

Such reforms were sufficient to end the immediate difficulties. But they were successful only temporarily because the reformers were allowed to act against only the results of the decay and not its cause, the continued monopoly of the self-interested ruling class. As soon as the worst consequences of decay had been alleviated, the old groups resumed power and their old ways. Moreover, the reformers did not understand that the Europe now faced by the Ottomans was far more powerful than that which the great sultans of the past had defeated; even if the reforms had been more permanently successful, they could not have corrected the increasing Ottoman weakness relative to the powerful nation-states then rising in Europe. Such an understanding was to come to the Ottoman reformers only in the 19th century.

Imperial Decline in the 18th and Early 19th Centuries

Most manifestations of decline were only continuations and elaborations of earlier conditions. In the later Ottoman period, however, a new factor of decline was added: the weakness of the central government resulted in the loss of control of most of the provinces to the local ruling notables, called *ayan* or *derebeyis* ("lords of the valley") in Anatolia and *klephts* or *hayduks* in Europe, who took more or less permanent control of large areas, creating a situation that in many ways resembled European feudalism much more than the traditional Ottoman *timar* system ever did. These notables were able to build up their power and maintain control not only because the sultan's government lacked the military resources to suppress them but also because the local populations preferred the notables' rule to that of the corrupt and incompetent Ottoman officials. In the Balkans and Anatolia local rulers solidified their positions by taking advantage of currents of local nationalism that were arising among the Balkan Christians. The notables formed private armies of mercenaries and slaves, which they sometimes used to provide important contributions to the Ottoman armies in return for recognition of their autonomy by the sultans. These rulers were able to exercise almost complete authority, collecting taxes for themselves and sending only nominal payments to the treasury, thus further increasing its problems. The central government maintained its position when it could by playing the local rebels against each other, using the leverage of Ottoman support to its own advantage and securing considerable payments of cash and military contributions when needed. The treasury, therefore, did not suffer as much from these provincial revolts as might be imagined, but the revolts did disrupt the established food supplies of the empire and caused large-scale famines to starve the major cities on a regular basis. In response, the urban populace became a restless, misruled, and anarchic mass that broke loose at the slightest provocation, responding to unemployment, famine, and plague with riots and summary executions of the officials considered responsible. This violence brought attention to Ottoman difficulties but did not remedy them and in fact made things worse. The potential for reform lay only in the hands of the ruling class, but its reaction was quite different.

Resistance to Change

Most Ottomans saw little need for the empire to change because they benefited financially from the anarchy and the sultan's lack of control. In addition, the ruling class was completely isolated from developments outside its own sphere; it assumed that the remedies to Ottoman decline lay entirely within Ottoman practice and experience. This resulted from the basic belief of Ottoman society in its own superiority over anything outsiders could possibly produce, a belief that had far more justification in the 16th century, when it arose, than in the 18th century. All the advances in industrial and commercial life, science and technology, and particularly political and military organization and techniques that had occurred in Europe since the Reformation were simply unknown to the Ottomans. The only direct Ottoman contacts with Europe were on the battlefield, where most Ottomans still assumed that their military reverses were caused not by the superiority of Western armies but rather by Ottoman failure to apply fully the techniques that had worked so well in the past. Thus, the 18th-century reforms largely paralleled those of the traditional Ottoman reformers of the 17th century, with only occasional efforts to add new military organizations and to make use of specific European weapons and techniques of undeniable superiority.

The destruction of the old army was completed in 1831 by the final abolition of the *timar* system, based on reforms instituted by Sultan Mahmud II as part of his program to create a modern Western-style army. The remaining *timars* were resumed by the government. The distinctively military aspects of the *timar* system were gradually transformed in some areas into the *çiftlik* system, which more closely resembled proprietorship over land. This process involved the severing of the peasantry from their traditional rights on the land and a corresponding creation of large estates farmed on a commercial basis.

CHAPTER 7

INTERPRETING FEUDAL CONCEPTS

T hose who formulated the concept of feudalism were affected by the search for simplicity and order in the universe associated with the work of Nicolaus Copernicus (1473–1543) and especially Isaac Newton (1642–1727). Historians and philosophers were persuaded that if the universe operated systematically, so, too, must societies. In the 16th century some students of the law and customs of the fief declared that feudal institutions were universal and maintained that feudal systems had existed in Rome, Persia, and Judaea. The philosopher Giambattista Vico (1668–1744) considered the fief one of humankind's eternal institutions. Adopting a similar position, Voltaire (1694–1778) contested the judgment of Montesquieu (1689–1755) that the appearance of feudal laws was a unique historical event.

The philosophical historians of 18th-century Scotland searched for feudalism outside western Europe, and they expanded the construct's field of significance to encompass peasants as well as lords. Adam Smith (1723–90) presented feudal government as a stage of social development characterized by the absence of commerce and by the use of semi-free labour to cultivate land. Smith's student John Millar (1735–1801) found "the outlines of the feudal policy" in Asia and

Portrait of Adam Smith, one of several 18th-century philosophical historians to examine and explain feudal constructs. Fine Art Images/SuperStock

Africa. The association popularly made between the feudal construct and ignorance and barbarism fostered its extension to regions that Europeans scarcely knew and that they considered backward and primitive.

Following Millar's precedent, some later historians continued to look for feudal institutions in times and places outside medieval Europe, most notably Japan. These efforts, predictably, resulted in misconceptions and misunderstanding. Historians using the feudal model for comparative purposes emphasized those characteristics that resemble or seem to resemble Western feudal practices and neglected other, dissimilar aspects, some of that were uniquely significant in shaping the evolution of the areas in question. For Westerners, the use of the feudal model necessarily created a deceptive sense of familiarity with societies that are different from their own.

Feudalism in the 19th and 20th Centuries

In the 19th century, influenced by Adam Smith and other Scottish thinkers, Karl Marx (1818–83) and Friedrich Engels (1820–95) made "the feudal mode of production" one stage in their visionary reading of Western historical development; the feudal model followed "the ancient mode of production" and preceded capitalism, socialism, and communism. Marx and Engels rejected the traditional understanding of feudalism as consisting of fiefs and relations among the elite and emphasized the lords' exploitation of the peasants as the essence of the feudal mode of production. Marx and Engels did not try to establish that the feudal period had existed universally; they formulated for Asia the idea of a specific Asiatic mode of production. Still, by incorporating "the feudal

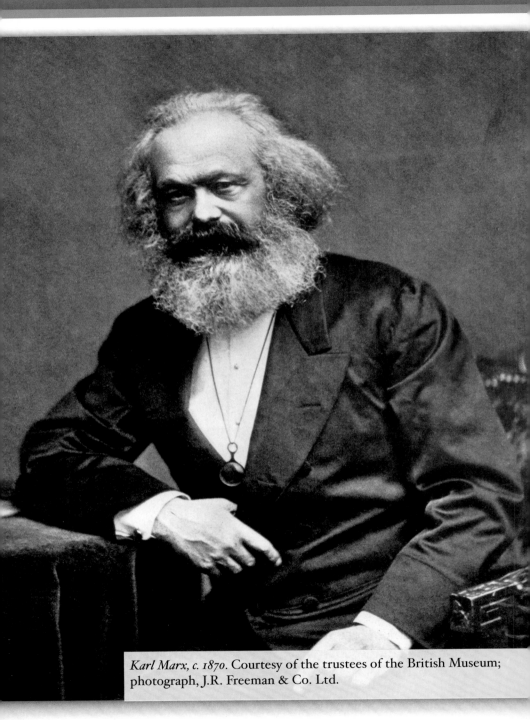

Karl Marx, c. 1870. Courtesy of the trustees of the British Museum; photograph, J.R. Freeman & Co. Ltd.

mode of production" into their design, they endowed it with seminal significance. Their followers came to view the feudal stage as a necessary prerequisite for the emergence of social-ism, and socialist scholars and activists sought traces of it throughout the world.

Marx and Engels's model of Western historical develop-ment indicates how popular the feudal construct had become by the middle of the 19th century. Their modification of the construct to serve their own purposes demonstrates its pliancy. However, they were not unique in having shaped the feudal con-struct to suit their particular perspective. The Australian medi-eval historian John O. Ward isolated 10 different sets of phe-nomena that historians had associated with feudalism. Some employed narrow legalistic definitions like those elaborated by 16th-century lawyers. Others, following the English historian Thomas Madox (1666–1726/27) and the French historian Marc Bloch (1886–1944), equated feudalism with feudal society. They saw feudalism as encompassing many if not most aspects of medieval society: peasants, whether free, unfree, or semi-free; a ruling warrior class with subordinates compensated for military service by grants of land rather than money; fragmentation of power; and disorder—yet with the family and the state retain-ing their importance. The American historian Joseph R. Strayer (1904–87) laid special emphasis on the splintering of political and public power and authority, and he believed that system-atized feudal institutions and customs were compatible with the formation of large political units, which he viewed as rec-ognizable precursors of contemporary nation-states. Although Bloch and Strayer employed the feudal construct throughout their careers, both admitted the idiosyncrasy of the various definitions of the feudal labels that have been proposed, and both acknowledged that focusing on the construct inevitably obscures the human beings, both individuals and groups, whose actions historians are dedicated to comprehending.

Modern Critiques

From the time of the French historian Louis Chantereau Le Febvre (1588–1658), questions were raised concerning the extent to which the feudal construct oversimplified and distorted the historical realities it was intended to capture. Chantereau Le Febvre denounced as futile the attempts of his contemporaries to deduce general rules from uncertain principles. He stressed the necessity of studying authentic acts and working "historically," implying thereby that his contemporaries were not working in this fashion. He cautioned against reducing the great variety of fiefs to a single type, because each fief was different from the others. Despite Chantereau Le Febvre's reservations, in the end he succumbed to current fashion and endorsed a simplified picture of feudal institutions. He did, however, edit and publish medieval documents demonstrating the difficulty of attaching precise meanings to such words as "feudum" and "allodium."

Many modern historians have attempted to follow Chantereau Le Febvre's admonitions and have studied these words and others, such as *vassus* ("vassal"), *homo* ("man"), and *fidelis* ("the faithful"), which figured centrally in the classic definitions of the feudal construct. By examining the contexts in which key words appear in a host of medieval acts and chronicles, they have demonstrated the wide range of meanings these words possessed and the difficulty of formulating simple and precise definitions of any of them. It is clear that in the Middle Ages those who fought (like those who farmed) were rewarded in different ways and were sometimes paid in money. Land was owned, controlled, and held in a variety of ways. Similarly, enterprising individuals used a range of tactics to augment their lands and wealth and increase their power. Standardization and regularization of tenurial and territorial bonds and of ceremonies such as homage accompanied the development of centralized government, as lords and kings used these devices (and many others) to buttress and extend their authority.

The extent to which surrender of property to a lord as a fief limited control and rights over the property has been investigated, as has the importance of such acts in creating ties between family groups that could be repeatedly renewed. The difficulty and danger of drawing sharp distinctions between the ceremonial practices of the nobility and the peasantry have been recognized, so, too, the importance of urban and parochial communities and the significance of spiritual and economic links between religious establishments and the laity. In studying the settlement of disputes, historians have emphasized the continuing importance of mediation and of judgments given by free men, especially members of the secular and ecclesiastical elite. Lordship has emerged as a more centrally important topic than the *feudum*. The quality of lords' relationships with their dependents, free and unfree, has been debated, with some historians stressing the predatory, exploitative aspects of lordship and others emphasizing its protective, beneficial features.

Increased knowledge of the Middle Ages and greater sophistication regarding the constructs (and periods) that scholars have created in attempting to comprehend the past have sparked the search for appropriate terms to describe human institutions and societies. Although the feudal labels have lost their validity as terms to designate the realities of medieval society, they provide insight into the thought processes and assumptions of the lawyers and historians who formulated and used them between the 16th and the 20th centuries.

CONCLUSION

Most national societies have passed through a stage in their social and political development, usually referred to as feudalism, in which a weak and ineffectively organized national government competes for territorial jurisdiction with local power holders. In medieval England and France, for example, the crown was perennially threatened by the power of the feudal nobles, and a protracted struggle was necessary before the national domain was subjected to full royal control.

Elsewhere, innumerable societies continued to experience this kind of feudal conflict between local magnates and the central government well into the modern era. The warlords of 19th- and 20th-century China, for example, were just as much the products of feudal society as the warring barons of 13th-century England and presented the same kind of challenge to the central government's claim to exercise sovereign jurisdiction over the national territory.

By the 1970s, feudalism was almost extinct. The social patterns that had formerly supported the power of local landowners were rapidly disappearing, and central governments had generally acquired a near monopoly of communications and military technology, enabling them to project their power into areas once controlled by local rulers.

allodium Land freely held, without obligation of service to any overlord.

aristocracy A governing body or upper class usually made up of a hereditary nobility.

benefice A form of medieval land tenure where a lord leased land to a freeman under a long-term payment plan

breach Failure to do what is required by agreement or law.

demesne Manorial land actually possessed by the lord and not held by tenants.

dynasty A family of rulers who rule over a country for a long period of time.

fief A large area of land that was ruled over by a lord in medieval times.

gentry Members of a class who are entitled to bear a coat of arms though not of noble rank.

hierarchy A system in which people or things are placed in a series of levels with different importance or status.

manorialism A political, economic, and social system by which the peasants of medieval Europe were tied to their land and their lord through serfdom.

monarchy Undivided rule or absolute sovereignty over a nation by a single person.

noble Of, relating to, or belonging to the highest social class.

parochial Of or relating to a church parish and the area around it.

peerage People who are members of the British nobility.

secular Of, relating to, or controlled by the government rather than by the church.

serf A member of a servile feudal class bound to the land and subject to the will of its owner.

socage A tenure of land by agricultural service fixed in amount and kind or by payment of money rent only and not burdened with any military service.

sovereign One possessing or held to possess supreme political power, such as a king or queen.

subsistence The amount of food, money, etc., that is needed to stay alive.

succession The conditions under which one person after another takes possession of property, title, or throne.

suzerain A dominant state controlling the foreign relations of a vassal state but allowing it sovereign authority in its internal affairs.

tenure The right to use property.

theocrat One who rules or lives under a form of government in which a country is ruled by religious leaders.

vassal A person under the protection of a feudal lord to whom he has vowed homage and fealty.

villein An unfree peasant standing as the slave of a feudal lord but free in legal relations with respect to all others.

BIBLIOGRAPHY

Feudalism (General)

Elizabeth A.R. Brown, "The Tyranny of a Construct: Feudalism and Historians of Medieval Europe, *The American Historical Review*, 79(4): 1063–88 (October 1974), is a foundational work. F.L. Ganshof, *Feudalism*, 3rd ed. (1964, reissued 1996; originally published in French, 2nd ed., 1947), is a traditional treatment. Marc Bloch, *Feudal Society*, 2 vol. (1961, reprinted 1989; originally published in French, 2 vol., 1939–40), is a classic study that defines feudalism as encompassing all aspects of society. Susan Reynolds, *Fiefs and Vassals: The Medieval Evidence* (1994), provides the most complete critique of the concept. Thomas N. Bisson (ed.), *Cultures of Power: Lordship, Status, and Process in Twelfth-Century Europe* (1995); Otto Brunner, *Land and Lordship: Structures of Governance in Medieval Austria* (1992; originally published in German, 4th rev. ed., 1959); and Guy Fourquin, *Lordship and Feudalism in the Middle Ages* (1976; originally published in French, 1970), are important studies of lordship and the relations between lords and their subjects that employ the traditional constructs. Useful studies of "bastard feudalism" are P.R. Cross, "Bastard Feudalism Revised," *Past and Present*, 125: 27–64 (November 1989); and Michael Hicks, *Bastard Feudalism* (1995).

Monarchy

The conditions that gave rise to monarchies are portrayed in Fernand Braudel, *A History of Civilizations* (1994; originally

163

published in French, 1987); Karl A. Wittfogel, *Oriental Despotism: A Comparative Study of Total Power* (1957, reprinted 1981); and C. Northcote Parkinson, *The Evolution of Political Thought* (1958). Theoretical discussions appear in S.N. Eisenstadt, *The Political Systems of Empires* (1963, reprinted 1993), which analyzes the political systems of the Classical empire-monarchies. J.H. Burns (ed.), *The Cambridge History of Medieval Political Thought, c. 350–c. 1450* (1988, reissued 1991); and J.H. Burns and Mark Goldie (eds.), *The Cambridge History of Political Thought, 1450–1700* (1991), include valuable articles about the ideologies legitimizing European monarchies.

Richard Bonney (ed.), *The Rise of the Fiscal State in Europe, c. 1200–1815* (1999); Catherine Mulgan, *The Renaissance Monarchies, 1469–1558* (1998); Michael S. Kimmel, "The Ambivalence of Absolutism: State and Nobility in 17th Century France and England," *Journal of Political and Military Sociology*, 14(1)55–74 (Fall 1986); and Max Beloff, *The Age of Absolutism, 1660–1815* (1954, reissued 1971), explain how monarchs used new technological, administrative, and propaganda tools to strengthen their rule while reaching compromises with nobility.

Discussions of monarchy and revolution are presented in Theda Skocpol, *States and Social Revolutions* (1979), one of the most convincing analyses of the fall of the absolutist French, Russian, and Chinese monarchies; Guglielmo Ferrero, *The Principles of Power: The Great Political Crises of History*, trans. by Theodore R. Jaeckel (1942; originally published in French, 1942), a classic about monarchies' attempts to cope with revolutionary tides, mostly in the 19th century; and Arno J. Mayer, *The Persistence of the Old Regime, Europe to the Great War* (1981), which advances the view that the social and cultural fabric of monarchical regimes remained intact until World War I.

Social and ceremonial aspects of monarchy are covered in Reinhard Bendix, *Kings or People: Power and the Mandate to Rule* (1978); and Norbert Elias, *The Court Society*, rev. ed. (2006; originally published in German, 1969). Samuel P. Huntington, *Political Order in Changing Societies* (1968, reprinted 2006), explains the collapse of colonial and ancient regimes in the Third World and how traditional monarchies are challenged by new forces. Joseph Kostiner (ed.), *Middle East Monarchies: The Challenge of Modernity* (2000), stresses how monarchy prevailed as the most popular political regime in the Arab world.

Territorial Monarchies (the Middle Ages)

Useful reference works are *The New Cambridge Medieval History*, 7 vol. (1995–2005); *Dictionary of the Middle Ages*, 13 vol. (1982–89); and *Encyclopedia of the Middle Ages*, 2 vol. (2000). A good outline of events in the Middle Ages is R.L. Storey, *Chronology of the Medieval World, 800–1491* (1973). Biographies of some important historians can be found in Helen Damico and Joseph Zavadil (eds.), *Medieval Scholarship: Biographical Studies in the Formation of a Discipline*, 3 vol. (1995–99). Two important volumes that represent scholarly perspectives of the late 20th and early 21st century are Peter Linehan and Janet L. Nelson, *The Medieval World* (2001); and Lester K. Little and Barbara Rosenwein (eds.), *Debating the Middle Ages: Issues and Readings* (1998).

Terminology and periodization are discussed in Fred C. Robinson, "Medieval, the Middle Ages," *Speculum*, 59(4):745–756 (October 1984); William A. Green, "Periodization in European and World History," *Journal of World History*, 3(1):13–53 (Spring 1992); Donald R. Kelley, *Foundations of Modern Historical Scholarship: Language, Law, and History in the French Renaissance* (1970); Lionel Gossman, *Medievalism and the Ideologies of the Enlightenment: The World and Work of La Curne de Sainte-Palaye* (1968); Jacques Le Goff, "The Several Middle Ages of Jules Michelet," in his *Time, Work, and Culture in the Middle Ages* (1980), pp. 3–28; Jacques Heers, *Le Moyen Âge, une imposture* (1992); Timothy Reuter, "Medieval: Another Tyrannous Construct?," *The Medieval History Journal*, 1(1):25–45 (1998), and other articles in the same number. Stuart Airlie, "Strange Eventful Histories: The Middle Ages in the Cinema," chapter 10 in Peter Linehan and Janet L. Nelson, *The Medieval World* (2001), pp. 163–183, provides an introduction to depictions of the Middle Ages in film.

German Feudalism

Patrick J. Geary, *Before France and Germany: The Creation and Transformation of the Merovingian World* (1988), examines the period from the perspective of the unity of late antiquity. Rosamond McKitterick, *The Frankish Kingdoms Under the Carolingians, 751–987* (1983), presents a general survey of Carolingian Europe, with an emphasis on cultural history.

G. Barraclough, *The Origins of Modern Germany*, 3rd ed. (1988), is a good analysis of medieval German history. General surveys include Alfred Haverkamp, *Medieval Germany, 1056–1273*, 2nd ed. (1992; originally published in German, 1984); and Timothy Reuter, *Germany in the Early Middle Ages*, c. 800–1056 (1991). K.J. Leyser, *Rule and Conflict in an Early Medieval Society: Ottonian Saxony* (1979, reissued 1989), explores the main forces of development of the Saxon empire and its society from 900 to 1024, and Leyser's *Medieval Germany and Its Neighbours, 900–1250* (1982) studies warfare, the nobility, and German-Byzantine and German-English relations.

A comprehensive German-language survey covering the Middle Ages is Friedrich Prinz, *Grundlagen und Anfänge: Deutschland bis 1056*, 2nd ed., rev. (1993).

Joachim Leuschner, *Germany in the Late Middle Ages* (1980; originally published in German, 1975), provides a basic introduction to political history. Studies of regional and local developments include Philippe Dollinger, *The German Hansa*, trans. and ed. by D.S. Ault and H. Steinberg (1970, reissued 1999; originally published in French, 1964); and Otto Brunner, *Land and Lordship: Structures of Governance in Medieval Austria*, trans. by Howard Kaminsky and James Van Horn Melton (1992; trans. from the German 4th, rev. ed., 1959). A valuable supplement is the more complex F.R.H. Du Boulay, *Germany in the Later Middle Ages* (1983).

An excellent guide is Thomas A. Brady, Jr., Heiko A. Oberman, and James D. Tracy (eds.), *Handbook of European History, 1400–1600: Late Middle Ages, Renaissance, and Reformation*, 2 vol. (1994–95). Bob Scribner and Sheilagh Ogilvie (eds.), *Germany: A New Social and Economic History*, 2 vol. (1996), is a good collection on the society and economy of the Renaissance and Reformation. Peter Blickle, *The Revolution of 1525: The German Peasants' War from a New Perspective* (1981, reissued 1985; originally published in German, 1975), stresses the common grievances that brought peasants and the urban poor together in what the author calls "the revolution of the common man."

French Feudalism

A comprehensive introduction is found in J.M. Wallace-Hadrill, *The Barbarian West, 400–1000*, 3rd rev. ed. (1998). On the Merovingians, see the engaging overview in Patrick J. Geary, *Before France and Germany* (1988), and J.M. Wallace-

Hadrill, *The Long-Haired Kings and Other Studies in Frankish History* (1962, reprinted 1982). For the Carolingians, see Pierre Riché, *The Carolingians: A Family Who Forged Europe* (1993; originally published in French, 1983); and F.L. Ganshof, *The Carolingians and the Frankish Monarchy*, trans. from French and German (1971). Special studies of the civilization of the period include J.M. Wallace-Hadrill, *The Frankish Church* (1983); Pierre Riché, *Education and Culture in the Barbarian West, Sixth Through Eighth Centuries* (1976; originally published in French, 3rd ed., 1962); Suzanne Fonay Wemple, *Women in Frankish Society: Marriage and the Cloister, 500 to 900* (1981, reprinted 1985); and Georges Duby, *The Early Growth of the European Economy: Warriors and Peasants from the Seventh to the Twelfth Century* (1974, reissued 1978; originally published in French, 1973).

The early Middle Ages as a whole is well treated in Jean Dunbabin, *France in the Making, 843–1180* (1985). The political history of this and the succeeding periods is surveyed best in Elizabeth M. Hallam and Judith Everard, *Capetian France, 987–1328*, 2nd ed. (2001); but Robert Fawtier, *The Capetian Kings in France: Monarchy & Nation, 987–1328* (1960, reissued 1982; originally published in French, 1942), is still a useful classic. Social change and feudalization are studied in Marc Bloch, *Feudal Society* (1961, reprinted 1989; originally published in French, 1939–40), a seminal work. An alternative to Bloch's model has been developed by Georges Duby, *La Société aux XIe et XIIe siècles dans la région mâconnaise* (1953, reissued 1988), and *The Three Orders: Feudal Society Imagined* (1980; originally published in French, 1978). Dominique Barthelemy, *La Mutation de l'an mil, a-t-elle eu lieu?: servage et chevalerie dans la France des Xe et XIe siècles* (1997), is also important.

For the general political history, see the works of Hallam and Fawtier in the previous section. Individual reigns are studied in John W. Baldwin, *The Government of Philip Augustus: Foundations of French Royal Power in the Middle Ages* (1986); and William Chester Jordan, *Louis IX and the Challenge of the Crusade: A Study in Rulership* (1979). For economy and society, see Georges Duby, *Rural Economy and Country Life in the Medieval West* (1968, reprinted 1998; originally published in French, 1962). Social unrest is discussed in Michel Mollat and Philippe Wolff, *The Popular Revolutions of the Late Middle Ages* (1973; originally published in French, 1970). Charles Petit-Dutaillis, *The French Communes in the Middle Ages* (1978; originally published in French, 1947), remains the standard account on the cities and towns.

England from 1066 to 1485

Translation of a wide range of sources, with commentary, can be found in David C. Douglas and George W. Greenaway (eds.), *English Historical Documents, 1042–1189* (1953); Harry Rothwell (ed.), *English Historical Documents, 1189–1327* (1975); and A.R. Myers (ed.), *English Historical Documents, 1327–1485* (1969), all from the above-mentioned series. Other good anthologies are R. Allen Brown, *The Norman Conquest* (1984); Bertie Wilkinson, *The Constitutional History of England, 1216–1399*, 3 vol. (1948–58, reprinted as *The Constitutional History of Medieval England, 1216–1399*, 1965–67), and *Constitutional History of England in the Fifteenth Century, 1399–1485* (1964). General works recommended include Helen M. Cam, *England Before Elizabeth*, 3rd ed. (1967); Austin Lane Poole, *From Domesday Book to Magna Carta, 1087–1216*, 2nd ed. (1955, reprinted 1998); Maurice Powicke, *The Thirteenth Century, 1216–1307*, 2nd ed. (1962); M.T. Clanchy, *England and Its Rulers, 1066–1272: Foreign Lordship and National Identity* (1983); May McKisack, *The Fourteenth Century, 1307–1399* (1959, reprinted 1992); Anthony Tuck, *Crown and Nobility 1272–1461: Political Conflict in*

Late Medieval England (1985); Michael Prestwich, *The Three Edwards: War and State in England, 1272–1377* (1980); E.F. Jacob, *The Fifteenth Century, 1399–1485* (1961, reprinted 1993); and M.H. Keen, *England in the Later Middle Ages: A Political History* (1973). Among studies of individual reigns are David C. Douglas, *William the Conqueror: The Norman Impact upon England*, new ed. (1999); Frank Barlow, *William Rufus* (1983); R.H.C. Davis, *King Stephen, 1135–1154* (1967, reissued 1977); W.L. Warren, *Henry II* (1973); Michael Prestwich, *Edward I* (1988); G.L. Harriss (ed.), *Henry V: The Practice of Kingship* (1985); Bertram Wolffe, *Henry VI* (1973); Charles Ross, *Edward IV* (1974, reprinted 1999), and *Richard III* (1981, reprinted 1988). The history of government and administration are considered in W.L. Warren, *The Governance of Norman and Angevin England, 1086–1272* (1987); S.B. Chrimes, *An Introduction to the Administrative History of Mediaeval England*, 3rd ed. (1966); and T.F. Tout, *Chapters in the Administrative History of Mediaeval England: The Wardrobe, the Chamber, and the Small Seals*, 6 vol. (1920–33, reprinted 1967).

Recommended works on special topics include R. Allen Brown, *The Normans and the Norman Conquest*, 2nd ed. (1985); V.H. Galbraith, *The Making of Domesday Book* (1961), superseded in many ways, but a classic; and Peter Sawyer (ed.), *Domesday Book: A Reassessment* (1985). Feudal society is the subject of Frank Stenton, *The First Century of English Feudalism, 1066–1166*, 2nd ed. (1961, reprinted 1979); Austin Lane Poole, *Obligations of Society in the XII and XIII Centuries* (1946, reprinted 1984); and J.C. Holt, *Magna Carta* (1965), the best account of the Great Charter. Also useful is J.C. Holt, *Magna Carta and Medieval Government* (1985). Studies of the nobility include K.B. McFarlane, *The Nobility of Later Medieval England* (1973, reprinted 1997), a most influential book; and Chris Given-Wilson, *The English Nobility in the Late Middle Ages: The Fourteenth-Century Politi-*

cal Community (1987). Parliament is studied in G.O. Sayles, *The King's Parliament of England* (1974); G.L. Harriss, *King, Parliament, and Public Finance in Medieval England to 1369* (1975); E.B. Fryde and Edward Miller (ed.), *Historical Studies of the English Parliament*, 2 vol. (1970); and R.G. Davies and J.H. Denton (eds.), *The English Parliament in the Middle Ages* (1981). The economy of the period is characterized in J.L. Bolton, *The Medieval English Economy, 1150–1500* (1980); Edward Miller and John Hatcher, *Medieval England: Rural Society and Economic Change, 1086–1348* (1978); M.M. Postan, *The Medieval Economy and Society: An Economic History of Britain in the Middle Ages* (1972); Reginald Lennard, *Rural England: 1086–1135: A Study of Social and Agrarian Conditions* (1959, reprinted 1966); and John Hatcher, *Plague, Population, and the English Economy, 1348–1530* (1977). England's major trade is discussed in Eileen Power, *The Wool Trade in English Medieval History* (1941, reprinted 1987); and T.H. Lloyd, *The English Wool Trade in the Middle Ages* (1977). Also informative are Susan Reynolds, *An Introduction to the History of English Medieval Towns* (1977, reprinted 1982); and Maurice Beresford, *New Towns of the Middle Ages: Town Plantation in England, Wales and Gascony* (1967, reprinted 1988). Studies of the church include Frank Barlow, *The English Church, 1066–1154: A History of the Anglo-Norman Church* (1979); David Knowles, *The Monastic Order in England: A History of Its Development from the Times of St. Dunstan to the Fourth Lateran Council, 940–1216*, 2nd ed. (1963), and *The Religious Orders in England*, 3 vol. (1948–59, reprinted 1979); W.A. Pantin, *The English Church in the Fourteenth Century* (1955, reprinted 1980); and C.H. Lawrence (ed.), *The English Church and the Papacy in the Middle Ages* (1965, reprinted 1984). Studies of the law of the period include Frederick Pollock and Frederic William Maitland, *The History of English Law Before the Time of Edward I*, 2nd ed., 2 vol. (1898, reissued 1982), still fundamental; Doris M. Stenton, *English Justice Between the Norman Conquest and the Great Charter, 1066–1215* (1964); Alan Harding, *The Law Courts of Medieval England* (1973); S.F.C. Milsom, *The Legal Framework of English Feudalism* (1976, reprinted 1986); and John Bellamy, *Crime and Public Order in England in the Later Middle Ages* (1973).

Italy in the Early Middle Ages

Comprehensive discussions of medieval Italy are provided in the first three volumes of *The Cambridge Medieval History: The Christian Roman Empire and the Foundation of the Teutonic Kingdoms*, 2nd ed., vol. 1 (1924, reprinted 1967); *The Rise of the Saracens and the Foundation of the Western Empire*, 2nd ed., vol. 2 (1924, reissued 1967); and *Germany and the Western Empire*, 2nd ed., vol. 3 (1924, reissued 1968). Giovanni Tabacco, *The Struggle for Power in Medieval Italy: Structures of Political Rule*, trans. by Rosalind Brown Jensen (1989; originally published in Italian, 1979), is a major survey of sociopolitical history. Also of interest is Chris Wickham, *Early Medieval Italy: Central Power and Local Society, 400–1000* (1981, reissued 1989).

Specific political and social topics of early periods are studied in T.S. Brown, *Gentlemen and Officers: Imperial Administration and Aristocratic Power in Byzantine Italy, A.D. 554–800* (1984) and Barbara M. Kreutz, *Before the Normans: Southern Italy in the Ninth and Tenth Centuries* (1991). Socioeconomic analyses include Bryan Ward-Perkins, *From Classical Antiquity to the Middle Ages: Urban Public Building in Northern and Central Italy, AD 300–850* (1984); and appropriate articles in Richard Hodges and Brian Hobley (eds.), *The Rebirth of Towns in the West, AD 700–1050* (1988). The art of this period is examined by Richard Krautheimer, *Rome,*

Profile of a City, 312–1308 (1980, reissued 2000); and Richard Hodges and John Mitchell (eds.), *San Vincenzo al Volturno: The Archaeology, Art, and Territory of an Early Medieval Monastery* (1985).

Italy in the 14th and 15th Centuries

General outlines of the period, together with references to important works in Italian and other languages, are to be found in Denys Hay and John Law, *Italy in the Age of the Renaissance, 1380–1530* (1989). An excellent work of reference is J.R. Hale (ed.), *A Concise Encyclopaedia of the Italian Renaissance* (1981). Wallace Klippert Ferguson, *The Renaissance in Historical Thought: Five Centuries of Interpretation* (1948, reprinted 1981), is useful for periodization.

China: The Zhou and Qin Dynasties

Useful works on the period include Nicola Di Cosmo, *Ancient China and Its Enemies: The Rise of Nomadic Power in East Asian History* (2002); Cho-yun Hsu (Zhouyun Xu) and Katheryn M. Linduff, *Western Chou Civilization* (1988); Mark Edward Lewis, *Sanctioned Violence in Early China* (1990); and Yu-ning Li, *The First Emperor of China* (1975); Xueqin Li, *Eastern Zhou and Qin Civilizations* (1986).

Medieval Japan

Among works of note on medieval Japan are several by Jeffrey P. Mass: *Warrior Government in Early Medieval Japan:*

A Study of the Kamakuru Bakufu, Shugo, and Jitō (1974, re-issued 1991), *The Development of Kamakura Rule, 1180–1250* (1979), and *Lordship and Inheritance in Early Medieval Japan: A Study of the Kamakura Soryō System* (1989). Excellent volumes of essays by Japanese and Western scholars include Jeffrey P. Mass (ed.), *Court and Bakufu in Japan: Essays in Kamakura History* (1982); John Whitney Hall and Jeffrey P. Mass (eds.), *Medieval Japan: Essays in Institutional History* (1974, reissued 1988); and John Whitney Hall and Toyoda Takeshi (Takeshi Toyoda) (eds.), *Japan in the Muromachi Age* (1977).

Other useful works include H. Paul Varley, *Imperial Restoration in Medieval Japan* (1971), and *Warriors of Japan as Portrayed in the War Tales* (1994); Minoru Shinoda, *The Founding of the Kamakura Shogunate, 1180–1185* (1960); Kenneth Allen Grossberg, *Japan's Renaissance: The Politics of the Muromachi Bakufu* (1981); Carl Steenstrup *Hōjō Shigetoki, 1198–1261, and His Role in the History of Political and Ethical Ideas in Japan* (1979); Peter Judd Arnesen, *The Medieval Japanese Daimyo: The Ōuchi Family's Rule of Suō and Nagato* (1979); Martin Collcutt, *Five Mountains: The Rinzai Zen Monastic Institution in Medieval Japan* (1981); Thomas Keirstead, *The Geography of Power in Medieval Japan* (1992); and Hitomi Tonomura, *Community and Commerce in Late Medieval Japan: The Corporate Villages of Tokuchin-ho* (1992).

Early Modern Japan (1550–1850)

Conrad Totman, *Early Modern Japan* (1993), is a good general text. Among the many excellent collections of essays are John Whitney Hall and Marius B. Jansen (eds.), *Studies in the Institutional History of Early Modern Japan* (1968); John Whitney Hall, Nagahara Keiji (Keiji Nagahara), and Kozo Yāmamura (eds.), *Japan Before Tokugawa: Political Consolidation and Economic Growth, 1500–1650* (1981; originally published in Japanese, 1978); Chie Nakane and Shinzaburō Ōishi (eds.), *Tokugawa Japan: The Social and Economic Antecedents of Modern Japan* (1990); and Tetsuo Najita and Irwin Scheiner (eds.), *Japanese Thought in the Tokugawa Period, 1600–1868: Methods and Metaphors* (1978, reissued 1988).

The Sengoku era is discussed in Mary Elizabeth Berry, *Hideyoshi* (1982), and *The Culture of Civil War in Kyoto* (1994); George Elison, *Deus Destroyed: The Image of Christianity in Early Modern Japan* (1973, reissued 1988); George Elison and Bardwell L. Smith (eds.), *Warlords, Artists & Commoners: Japan in the Sixteenth Century* (1981); and Neil McMullin, *Buddhism and the State in Sixteenth-Century Japan* (1984).

Classical Ottoman Society and Administration

Ottoman administration and society are treated in Joseph von Hammer (Joseph, Freiherr von Hammer-Purgstall), *Des Osmanischen Reichs Staatsverfassung und Staatsverwaltung*, 2 vol. (1815, reprinted 1977), a detailed study of Ottoman administrative organization in the 16th century. Hamilton Gibb and Harold Bowen, *Islamic Society and the West*, vol. 1 in 2 parts (1950), emphasizes Ottoman organization in the 18th century but adds considerable information on earlier periods based on examination of Turkish and Western sources. A.D. Alderson, *The Structure of the Ottoman Dynasty* (1956, reprinted 1982), details the Ottoman imperial institution and the development of the Ottoman dynasty. An exhaustive study of Ottoman political, economic, and social life in the 17th century is Robert Mantran, *Istanbul dans la seconde moitié du XVIIe siècle* (1962). Extensive accounts of popular customs are Suraiya Faroqhi, *Towns and Townsmen of Ottoman Anatolia: Trade, Crafts, and Food Production in an Urban Setting, 1520–1650* (1984); Bernard Lewis, *Istanbul and the Civilization of the Ottoman Empire* (1963, reissued 1972); Raphaela Lewis, *Everyday Life in Ottoman Turkey* (1971, reissued 1988); and Fanny Davis, *The Ottoman Lady: A Social History from 1718 to 1918* (1986). The Ottoman millet system is discussed in Stanford J. Shaw, *The Jews of the Ottoman Empire and the Turkish Republic* (1991); and Benjamin Braude and Bernard Lewis (eds.), *Christians and Jews in the Ottoman Empire*, 2 vol. (1982).

Decline of the Ottoman Empire

Walter Livingston Wright, Jr. (trans. and ed.), *Ottoman Statecraft* (1935, reissued 1971), is a 17th-century Ottoman analysis of decline. Thomas M. Barker, *Double Eagle and Crescent: Vienna's Second Turkish Siege and Its Historical Setting* (1967), is a detailed study of the Eastern question relative to the Ottoman Empire in the late 17th century. Lavender Cassels, *The Struggle for the Ottoman Empire, 1717–1740* (1966), discusses a similar topic in readable fashion. Mary Lucille Shay, *The Ottoman Empire from 1720 to 1734 as Revealed in Despatches of the Venetian Baili* (1944, reprinted 1978), describes Ottoman life during the Tulip Period, based on thereports of Venetian consuls in Istanbul. Heinrich Benedikt, *Der Pascha-Graf Alexander von Bonneval, 1675–1747* (1959); M.S. Anderson, *The Eastern Question, 1774–1923: A Study in International Relations* (1966, reprinted 1991), an outline of diplomacy; and Richard F. Kreutel (trans.), *Kara Mustafa vor Wien: 1683 aus der Sicht türkischer Quellen*, trans. from

Turkish, enlarged ed. prepared by Karl Teply (1982), are also of interest. Stanford J. Shaw, *Between Old and New: The Ottoman Empire Under Sultan Selim III, 1789–1807* (1971), is a detailed study of the Ottoman reform effort in the late 18th and early 19th centuries, with an account of the diplomatic and military relations with Europe and of problems in the Balkan, Anatolian, and Arab provinces.

INDEX